E. B. Pusey

Lent Readings from the Fathers

E. B. Pusey

Lent Readings from the Fathers

ISBN/EAN: 9783741194344

Manufactured in Europe, USA, Canada, Australia, Japa

Cover: Foto ©Andreas Hilbeck / pixelio.de

Manufactured and distributed by brebook publishing software (www.brebook.com)

E. B. Pusey

Lent Readings from the Fathers

Lent Readings

FROM

THE FATHERS

SELECTED FROM

THE LIBRARY OF THE FATHERS.

OXFORD,
JAMES PARKER & Co.;
AND 377, STRAND, LONDON.
MDCCCLXXII.

PREFACE.

THE intention which the Compiler had in view in making these extracts was not that of collecting mere "beauties" of The Fathers, or of illustrating any one particular subject, or of enforcing any favourite tone of doctrine, but simply that of affording a resting-place for the mind *in reading*.

It was thought that if each day of the sacred season of Lent were occupied on some one special subject, as treated by the Fathers in their own language, and without modern comment, it might help towards a more devotional tone of mind, and somewhat further in its degree the great end we all ought to have at heart, in recovering the ancient spirit of holy things in the English Church.

The works from which these extracts are made, even though in themselves translations, namely the "Library of the Fathers," published at Oxford, are still too voluminous, and contain matter too diffused and scattered as to subject, for the common readers of the world, and it may happen that the reading of some small portion of a treatise or a Sermon or a Homily here set forth may be successfully attempted by those who would never have the courage to peruse the larger volumes.

While again it may happen that some persons here and there, as yet ignorant of the very great value of the works in question, may be arrested by these passages and be carried on further and further in their perusal, so as to be led ultimately to a more systematic examination of the originals.

They will surely find that in proportion to the study which they bestow on such of the ancient authors as are here set forth, so will be their love of and adherence to the Church in which it has been our blessing to be baptized.

Whatever our practice may be, and however great our short-comings in the paths of the old English Catholic Church, still even yet, in theory at least, they will find that the English Church may be preferred above any other national Church (with the exception perhaps of the true Church of Scotland) as more in harmony with the Church of S. Chrysostom, S. Augustine, and S. Cyprian.

May all our labours (under God's Blessing) be directed to strengthening those who stand, and winning those who are yet without, so that at length the Churchmen of the former and the latter ages may be gathered together into one fold, as we have but One Shepherd.

W. I. E. B.

Frome, Conversion of S. Paul. 1852.

THE Editors of the Library of the Fathers have long wished to publish selections from them for devotional purposes, in the hope that their thoughtful and meditative teaching might find access to classes whose means do not enable them to possess themselves of the larger works. It is one thing to argue from the Fathers, in proof of doctrine; another, to listen to them as practical teachers, opening, as they do richly, the meaning of Holy Scripture, or impressing the substance of the great truths of the Gospel. To quote or argue from the Fathers requires learning; to learn of them, only teachableness. S. Chrysostom and S. Augustine preached to mixed congregations of the same average intellect and moral character as the various educated classes among ourselves. S. Augustine often takes especial pains to make himself clear, on any difficult subject, to those of slower understanding, and bids those of the cleverer sort wait for them. There seems then no reason why men or women, or even the poor among us, should not be taught by S. Augustine, to say the least, as well as by any, such as we are. There is nothing learned in this. It is people's own fault if they make a show of learning, or argue, in a shallow way, from this or that Father, whom they happen to hear alleged in controversy. The Fathers spoke to the hearts of their own people, the members of the One Body of Christ, in their own day; they will yet speak to the heart, if they are read with hearts which God teaches.

This selection has come, then, as a grateful contribution from one whose blessed influence in winning, by God's help, poor and rich to the love of Christ, will long be valued, when the recent storms will be remembered only to be deplored.

It will be followed, if God will, by selections for Advent, and perhaps by others. But each will form a whole by itself.

E. B. P.

Christ Church. Sexagesima. 1852.

CONTENTS.

I. ASH-WEDNESDAY . . *Penitence* . . S. Cyp.
II. I. THURSDAY . . *Worldly cares* . S. Chrys.
III. I. FRIDAY . . *The Temptation* Catena Aurea.
IV. I. SATURDAY . . *Vain-glory* . . S. Aug.
V. I. SUNDAY . . *Rejoicing always* . S. Chrys.
VI. I. MONDAY *Esteeming God more than man* ———
VII. I. TUESDAY . . *Good use of Time* . ———
VIII. II. WEDNESDAY . *Almsgiving* . . S. Aug.
IX. II. THURSDAY . *Danger of evil words* . S. Chrys.
X. II. FRIDAY . . . *Prayer* . . S. Aug.
XI. II. SATURDAY . . *Riches* . . S. Chrys.
XII. II. SUNDAY *The Holy Catholic Church* S. Cyril Jer.
XIII. II. MONDAY . *Faithful Stewardship* . S. Chrys.
XIV. II. TUESDAY . . *Example* . . ———
XV. III. WEDNESDAY . . *Fasting* . . ———
XVI. III. THURSDAY *Christ's Spiritual Cures* S. Aug.
XVII. III. FRIDAY . . *Repentance* . . S. Pacian.
XVIII. III. SATURDAY *Co-operation of virtues* S. Greg.
XIX. III. SUNDAY . *The Pool of Bethesda* . S. Aug.
XX. III. MONDAY { *Love and obedience better than miracles* } . S. Chrys.
XXI. III. TUESDAY . . *Meekness* . . ———
XXII. IV. WEDNESDAY *Taking up the Cross* . S. Aug.
XXIII. IV. THURSDAY. *Unity of the Church* . S. Cyp.
XXIV. IV. FRIDAY . . *Confession* . . S. Aug.

CONTENTS.

XXV. IV. SATURDAY	*Anger*	S. Chrys.
XXVI. IV. SUNDAY	*Right use of Lent*	——
XXVII. IV. MONDAY	*Christ asleep in the storm*	S. Aug.
XXVIII. IV. TUESDAY	*The good Physician*	——
XXIX. V. WEDNESDAY	*Preventing God's Judgments*	S. Chrys.
XXX. V. THURSDAY	*Christian Activity*	——
XXXI. V. FRIDAY	*The Yoke of Christ*	S. Aug.
XXXII. V. SATURDAY	*Long-suffering of God*	S. Chrys.
XXXIII. PASSION SUNDAY	*Thankfulness*	——
XXXIV. MONDAY IN PASSION WEEK	*Danger of Self-indulgence*	——
XXXV. TUESDAY	*Patience*	S. Cyp.
XXXVI. WEDNESDAY	*Humility*	S. Chrys.
XXXVII. THURSDAY	*True Wisdom*	——
XXXVIII. FRIDAY	*Tribulation*	S. Aug.
XXXIX. SATURDAY	*Unity*	S. Chrys.
XL. PALM SUNDAY	*The Christian's Hope*	S. Aug.
XLI. MONDAY IN HOLY WEEK	*Fear of Death*	S. Cyp.
XLII. TUESDAY	*The Cross of Christ*	S. Chrys.
XLIII. WEDNESDAY	*The King of the Jews*	S. Aug.
XLIV. MAUNDY THURSDAY	*Christ washing the disciples' feet*	——
XLV. GOOD FRIDAY	*The Crucifixion*	S. Cyril Jer.
XLVI. EASTER EVE	*Watching*	S. Ephrem.

Ash-Wednesday.

TRUE PENITENCE. S. CYPRIAN.

I ENTREAT you, most dear brethren, let each confess his sin, while the sinner is yet among the living, while his confession can be accepted, while the satisfaction and remission wrought by the priests are pleasing before the Lord. Let us turn to the Lord with the whole heart, and call down the mercy of God, by expressing repentance for our offence by genuine grief. Before Him let the soul be laid prostrate, with Him let our sadness gain peace, on Him all our hope be leant. How we ought to intreat, Himself teaches us. "Turn ye," saith He, "unto Me, with all your heart, and with fasting, and with weeping, and with mourning, and rend your hearts and not your garments," To the Lord let us return with all our heart. Let us appease His wrath and displeasure, with fastings, with weepings, with mournings, as Himself teaches. Are we to think that he makes lamentation with his whole heart, with fasting, weeping and mourning, who fattening on rich repasts, and swollen with abundant dainties, never give shares of his meat and drink for the necessity of the poor? Moving with gay and pleasant step, wherein does he weep over his ruin? Or if arrayed in costly garments, does he care to please others, who displeases God? Or is she weeping and lamenting who can find leisure to enrobe herself in precious raiment, without considering that robe of Christ which she has lost; and to take to her costly ornaments and elaborate necklaces, never weeping at the forfeiture of her divine and heavenly adorning? Naked thou art, though garbed in foreign draperies and silken robes. Studded with gold and pearls, and gems, still thou art unsightly, if Christ's Beauty is wanting. If thou hadst lost any friend thou lovest, parted away by death, thou wouldest groan in sadness and weep, and with disordered countenance, altered dress, hair neglected, gloomy looks, and dejected visage, wouldest express the indications of sorrow. It is thine own soul, wretched woman, that thou hast lost; the spiritual life gone, thou for a while leadest on a life of thine own, and movest about, wearing thy death upon thee, yet there is no bitter mourning, no groaning continual, thou dost not withdraw away, either from shame for thy guilt, or to prolong thy lamentation. Lo, wounds of sin more deep, and increased delinquency; to offend, nor do amends; to have fallen from duty, and not lament thy fall. Ananias, Azarias and Misael, the illustrious and noble children, refrained not from confession before God, even amid 'the flames and heat of the fiery furnace. Though having a good conscience, and with acceptance oftentimes acquired before the Lord, by submission of faith and fear, yet ceased they not to keep hold of their humility,.

and make amends to the Lord, even amidst the martyr glories of their high deeds. Divine Scripture saith, "Azarias stood up and prayed, and opening his mouth made confession before God, together with his companions, in the midst of the fire."

Daniel also, after the multiplied grace of his faith and innocence, after the good pleasure of the Lord, oftentimes shewn toward his virtues and praises, still endeavours to gain His acceptance by fasting; enwraps himself in sackcloth and ashes, sorrowfully making his confession, and saying, "O Lord God, Great and Strong, and Dreadful, keeping Thy covenant and mercy to them that love Thee, and to them that keep Thy Commandments; we have sinned and have committed iniquity, and done wickedly, and have transgressed, and departed from Thy precepts and from Thy judgments; neither have we hearkened to the words of Thy servants the prophets, which they spake in Thy Name, to our kings, and to all the nations and all the land. O Lord, righteousness belongeth unto Thee, but unto us confusion." These things did men, meek, simple, innocent in gaining acceptance of the Majesty of God; yet now those who have denied the Lord, draw back from seeking peace and intreating Him.

I beseech you, brethren, give way to wholesome remedies, and obey better counsels; join your tears with ours, and to our sighs add your own. We intreat you to make us able to intreat God for you: we first turn those prayers to yourselves, wherewith we would implore God's pity in your behalf. And yield not to that unwise error or vacant senselessness of some, who, when involved in sin, are stricken with blindness of mind, and can neither understand their sins nor lament them. This is the greater plague of a wrathful God; as it is written, "God gave them a spirit of deadness;" and again, "They received not the love of the truth that they might be saved; and for this cause God shall send them strong delusion, that they should believe a lie; that they all might be damned who believed not the truth, but had pleasure in unrighteousness." Pleasing themselves in unrighteousness, mad in the bewilderment of a deadened mind, they contemn the precepts of the Lord, neglect the remedy of their wound, and refuse to repent; unwise before they sinned, and obstinate after.

But you, dearest brethren, who have a ready fear to God-ward, and whose mind, even amid its fall, is conscious of its misery, do you in penitence and sorrow gain knowledge of your sins, recognise the deep charge upon your conscience, open the eyes of the heart to an intelligence of your offence, not despairing of the Lord's Mercy, yet neither making light claim to His pardon. God, as with the affection of a Father He is ever indulgent and kind, so with the majesty of a Judge is He dreadful. As we have sinned greatly, let us weep greatly. For a deep wound diligent and long tending must not be wanting; the repentance must not fall short of the offence.

If any man offer prayer with his whole heart,

if he groan in the true misery and tears of repentance, if by a continuance of good works, he bend the Lord to a pardon of his sin, He Who in these words expressed His tender mercy, will shew mercy to such a man; "When you turn and lament, then shall you be saved, and know where you have been." And again, "I have no pleasure in the death of the wicked," saith the Lord, "but that he turn from his way and live." And the Prophet Joel declares the graciousness of the Lord, by the Lord's own Word, "Turn ye," saith he, "to the Lord your God, for He is merciful and gracious, slow to anger and of great mercy, and repenteth Him toward the evil which He hath inflicted." He can shew indulgence; to the man who is penitent, who does good works, who intreats, He can graciously give pardon, He can impute whatever for such an one martyrs pray, and priests perform. Or if any one move Him yet further by his own satisfaction, if he appease His wrath, the displeasure of an angered God, by worthy supplication; He grants weapons again, wherewith the conquered may be armed, recruits and invigorates that strength, whereby his refreshed faith may be quickened. The warrior will return to his warfare, will renew the fight, will challenge the enemy, by his sufferings only made stronger for the conflict. He who has thus made satisfaction to God, who through repentance for what he has done, through shame for his sin, has gained to himself an increase, both of virtue and faith, from the very suffering which his fall occasions, heard and helped by the Lord, will bring gladness to the Church, whom he had grieved, and purchase not only God's pardon now, but a crown also.

De Laps. xix—xxii.

First Thursday in Lent.

WORLDLY CARES.   S. CHRYSOSTOM.

"CONSIDER the lilies of the field."

Hereby Christ teaches us not only to take no thought, but not even to be dazzled at the costliness of men's apparel. Why? such comeliness is of grass, such beauty of the green herb, or rather the grass is even more precious than such apparelling. Why then pride thyself on things, whereof the prize rests with the mere plant, with a great balance in its favour?

And in the end after its triumph "it is cast into the oven;" and if of things mean and worthless, and of no great use, God hath displayed so great care, how shall He give up thee, of all living creatures the most important.

Wherefore then did He make them so beautiful? That He might display His own Wisdom and the excellency of His Power, that from every thing we might learn His Glory. For not the Heavens only "declare the Glory of God," but the earth too, and this David declared when he said, " Praise the Lord ye fruitful trees and all cedars." For some by their fruits, some by their greatness, some by their beauty, send up praise to Him Who made them. If then to the grass He hath given that which it needs not, how shall He not give unto thee that which thou needest? If that which is the vilest of all things, He hath lavishly adorned, and that as doing it not for need, but for munificence, how much more will He honour thee the most honourable of all things, in matters which are of necessity.

Now when as you see, He had demonstrated the greatness of God's providential care, so they were in what follows to be rebuked also; yet even in this He was sparing, laying to their charge not want, but poverty of faith. Thus "if God," saith he, "so clothe the grass of the field, much more you, oh ye of little faith."

Now if for bare necessaries one is not to take thought, what pardon can we deserve, who take thought for things expensive? Or rather, what pardon can they deserve who do even without sleep, that they may take the things of others?

"Therefore take no thought saying, What shall we eat, or what shall we drink, or wherewithal shall we be clothed? For after all these things do the nations of the world seek." Seest thou how again He hath both shamed them the more, and hath also shewn by the way, that He had commanded nothing grievous or burdensome? As therefore when He said, " If ye love them that love you, it is nothing great which ye practise, for the very Gentiles do the same," by the mention of the Gentiles He was stirring them up to something greater; so now also He brings them forward to reprove us, and to signify that it is a necessary debt which He is requiring of us. For if we must shew forth something more than the Scribes or Pharisees, what can we deserve, who so far from going beyond these, do even abide in the mean estate of the Gentiles, and emulate their littleness of soul. He doth not however stop at the rebuke, but having by this reproved and roused them, and shamed them with all strength of expression, by another argument He also comforts them, saying, "For your Heavenly Father knoweth that ye have need of all these things." He said not, "God knoweth;" but "your Father knoweth;" to lead them to a greater hope. For if he be a Father, and such a Father, He will not surely be able to overlook His children, in extremity of evils: seeing that not even men, being fathers, bear to do so.

And He adds along with this yet another argument. Of what kind then is it? That "ye have need" of them. What He saith is like this; What! are these things superfluous that He should disregard them? Yet not even in superfluities did He shew Himself wanting in regard, in the instance of the grass; but now are these things even necessary. So that what thou considerest a cause for thy being anxious, this I say is sufficient to draw thee from such anxiety. I mean if thou sayest, "Therefore I must needs take thought, because they are necessary;" on the contrary, I say, "Nay, for this selfsame reason take no thought, because they are necessary." Since were they superfluities, not even then ought we to despair, but to feel confident about the supply of them; but now that they are necessary, we must no longer be in doubt. For what kind of father is he, who can endure to fail in supplying to his children even necessaries? So that for this cause again God will most surely bestow them.

For indeed He is the Artificer of our nature, and He knows perfectly the wants thereof. So that neither canst thou say, "He is indeed our Father, and the things we seek are necessary, but He knows not that we stand in need of them." For He that knows our nature itself, and was the Framer of it, and formed it such as it is, evidently He knows its need also better than thou, who art placed in want of them: it having been by His decree, that our nature is in such need. He will not therefore oppose Himself to what He hath willed, first subjecting it of necessity to so great want, and on the other hand depriving it of what it wants, and of absolute necessaries.

Let us not therefore be anxious, for we shall gain nothing by it, but tormenting ourselves. For whereas He gives both when we take thought, and when we do not, and more of the two when we do not; what dost thou gain by thy anxiety, but to exact of thyself a superfluous penalty? Since one on the point of going to a plentiful feast, will not surely permit himself to take thought for food, nor is he that is walking to a fountain anxious about drink. Therefore seeing we have a supply more copious than either any fountain, or innumerable banquets made ready, the Providence of God, let us not be beggars, nor little minded.

For together with this, He puts also yet another reason for feeling confidence about such things, saying, "Seek ye the kingdom of Heaven, and all these things shall be added unto you." Thus when He had set the soul free from anxiety, then He also made mention of Heaven. For indeed He came to do away with the old things, and to call us to a greater country. Therefore He doth all, to deliver us from things unnecessary, and from our affection for the earth. For this cause He mentioned the heathens also, saying that "the Gentiles seek after these things;" they whose whole labour is for the present life, who have no regard for the things to come, nor any thought of Heaven. But to you not these present are chief things, but other than these. For we were not born to this end, that we should eat and drink and be clothed, but that we might please God, and attain unto the good things to come. Therefore as things here are secondary in our labour, so also in our prayers let them be secondary. Therefore He also said, "Seek ye the kingdom of Heaven, and all these things shall be added unto you."

And He said not, "shall be given," but "shall be added," that thou mightest learn that the things present are no great part of His gifts, compared with the greatness of the things to come. Accordingly He doth not bid us so much as ask for them, but while we ask for other things, to have confidence, as though these also were added to those. Seek then the things to come, and thou wilt receive the things present also; seek not the things that are seen, thou shalt surely attain unto them. Yea, for it is unworthy of thee to approach thy Lord for such things. And thou, who oughtest to spend all thy zeal and thy care for those unspeakable blessings, dost greatly disgrace thyself by consuming it on the desire of transitory things.

"How then?" saith one, "did He not bid us ask for bread?" Nay, He added, daily; and to this again, this day; which same thing in fact He doth here also. For He said not, "take no thought," but "take no thought for the morrow;" at the same time both affording us liberty, and fastening our soul on those things that are more necessary for us.

For to this end also He bade us ask even those, not as though God needed reminding by us, but that we might learn that by His Help we accomplish whatever we do accomplish, and that we might be made more His Own by our continual prayer for these things.

Seest thou how by this again He would persuade them, that they shall surely receive the things present? For He that bestows the greater, much more will He give the less. "For not for this end," saith He, "did I tell you not to take thought, nor to ask, that ye should suffer distress, and go about naked, but in order that ye might be in abundance of these things also:" and this you see was suited above all things to attract them unto Him. So that like as in almsgiving when deterring them from making a display to men, He won upon them chiefly by promising to furnish them with it more liberally; "for thy Father," saith He, "Who seeth in secret, shall reward thee openly;" even so here also in drawing them off from seeking these things, this is His persuasive topic, that He promises to bestow it on them not seeking it in greater abundance. Thus to this end, saith He, do I bid thee not seek; not that thou mayest not receive, but that thou mayest receive plentifully, that thou mayest receive in the fashion that becomes thee, with the profit which thou oughest to have, that thou mayest not by taking thought and distracting thyself in anxiety about these, render thyself unworthy both of these, and of the things spiritual; that thou mayest not undergo unnecessary distress, and again fall away from that which is set before thee.

"Take therefore no thought for the morrow; for sufficient unto the day is the evil thereof;" that is to say, the affliction and the bruising thereof. Is it not enough for thee to eat thy bread in the sweat of thy face? why add the further affliction that comes of anxiety, when thou art on the point to be delivered henceforth even from the former toils?

By evil here He means, not wickedness, far from it, but affliction, and trouble, and calamities; much as in another place also He saith, "Is there evil in a city which the Lord hath not done?" (Amos iii. 6,) not meaning rapines, nor injuries, nor anything like these, but the scourges which are borne from above. And again, "I," saith He, "make peace and create evil." (Isa. xlv. 7.)

This then is His meaning here also, when He saith, "Sufficient unto the day is the evil thereof." For nothing so pains the soul as carefulness and anxiety. Thus did Paul also, when urging to celibacy, give counsels, saying, "I would have you without carefulness."

Mark His tender care also, how He surpasses the affection of any father. "This I command," saith He, "for nothing else, but that I may deliver you from superfluous anxieties. For even if to-day thou hast taken thought for to-morrow, thou wilt also have to take thought again to-morrow. Why then, what is our labour? Why force the day to receive more than the distress which is allotted to it, and together with its own troubles add to it also the burden of the following day; and this when there is no chance of thy lightening the other by the addition so taking place, but thou art merely to exhibit thyself as courting superfluous troubles?"

Nevertheless, after so many grave words, we take thought for these things, but for the things in Heaven no longer; rather we have reversed His order, on either side fighting against His sayings. For mark, "Seek ye not the things present," saith He, "at all;" but we are seeking these things for ever. "Seek the things in Heaven," saith He; but those things we seek not so much as for a short hour, but according to the greatness of the anxiety we display about the things of the world, and the carelessness we entertain in things spiritual, or rather even much greater. But this doth not prosper for ever, neither can this be for ever.

Homil. in S. Matt. xxii.

First Friday in Lent.
THE TEMPTATION.

"THEN was Jesus led up of the Spirit into the wilderness to be tempted of the devil."

The Lord being baptized by John with water, is led by the Spirit into the wilderness to be baptized by the fire of temptation. Whoever thou art then that after thy baptism sufferest grievous trials, be not troubled thereat; for this thou receivedst arms to fight, not to sit idle. God does not hold all trial from us; first, that we may feel that we are become stronger; secondly, that we may not be puffed up by the greatness of the gifts we have received; thirdly, that the devil may have experience that we have entirely renounced him; fourthly, that by it we may be made stronger; fifthly, that we may receive a sign of the treasure intrusted to us; for the devil would not come upon us to tempt us, did he not see us advanced to great honours. The devil's snares are chiefly spread for the sanctified, because a victory over the saints is more desired than over others.

Why did Christ offer Himself to temptation? That He might be our Mediator in vanquishing temptation, not by aid only, but by example. He was led, not against His will, or as a prisoner, but as by a desire for the conflict. The devil comes against men to tempt them, but since he could not come against Christ, therefore Christ came against the devil. We should know that there are three modes of temptation; suggestion, delight, and consent; and we when we are tempted commonly fall into delight or consent, because being born of the sin of the flesh, we bear with us whence we afford strength for the contest, but God Who Incarnate of the Virgin's womb came into the world without sin, carried within Him nothing of a contrary nature. He could then be tempted by suggestion, but the delight of sin never gnawed His Soul, and therefore all that temptation of the devil was without, not within Him.

And that you may learn how great a good is fasting, and what a mighty shield against the devil, and that after baptism you ought to give attention to fasting and not to lusts, therefore Christ fasted, not Himself needing it, but teaching us by His Example. And to fix the measure of our quadragesimal fast He fasted forty days and forty nights; therefore we also in the season of Lent, as much as in us lies, afflict our flesh by abstinence.

Now let us shortly review what is signified by Christ's temptations. The fasting is abstinence from things evil, hunger is the desire of evil, bread is the gratification of the desire. He who indulges himself in any evil thing, turns stones into bread. Let him answer to the devil's persuasions that man does not live by the indulgences of desire alone, but by keeping the commands of God. When any is puffed up as though he were holy he is led to the temple, and when he esteems himself to have reached the summit of holiness he is set on a pinnacle of the temple. And this temptation follows the first, because victory over temptation begets conceit. But observe that Christ had voluntarily undertaken the fasting, but was led to the temple by the devil; therefore do you voluntarily use praiseworthy abstinence, but suffer yourself not to be exalted to the summit of sanctity; fly highmindedness, and you will not suffer a fall. The ascent of the mountain is the going forward to great riches, and the glory of this world, which springs from pride of heart. When you desire to become rich, that is, to ascend the mountain, you begin to think of the ways of gaining wealth and honours, and then the prince of this world is shewing you the glory of his kingdom. In the third place he provides you reasons, that if you seek to obtain all these things, you should serve him, and neglect the righteousness of God. When we have overcome the devil and bruised his head, we see that angels' ministry and the offices of heavenly virtues will not be wanting to us.

CATENA AUREA—
S. Matt. cap. iv.
SS. Chrys., Hilary, Aug., Jerom, Greg.

First Saturday in Lent.

VAIN-GLORY. S. AUGUSTINE.

IT is wont to perplex many persons, dearly beloved, that our Lord Jesus Christ in His evangelical sermon, after He had first said, "Let your light so shine before men, that they may see your good works, and glorify your father which is in heaven," said afterwards, " Take heed that ye do not your righteousness before men to be seen of them." For so the mind of him who is weak in understanding is disturbed, as desirous to obey both precepts, and distracted by diverse and contradictory commandments. For a man can as little obey but one master, if he give contradictory orders, as he can serve two masters, which the Saviour Himself hath testified in the same sermon to be impossible. What then must the mind that is in this hesitation do, when it thinks that it cannot, and yet is afraid not to obey ? For if he set his good works in the light to be seen of men, that he may fulfil the command, "Let your light so shine before men, that they may see your good works, and glorify your Father which is in heaven;" he will think himself involved in guilt because he has done contrary to the other precept which says, "Take heed that ye do not your righteousness before men to be seen of them." And again, if fearing and avoiding this, he conceal his good works, he will think that he is not obeying Him Who commands, saying, "Let your light shine before men, that they may see your good works."

But he who is of a right understanding, fulfils both, and will obey in both the Universal Lord of all, Who would not condemn the slothful servant, if He commanded those things which could by no means be done. For give ear to "Paul, the servant of Jesus Christ, called to be an apostle, separated unto the Gospel of God," both doing and teaching both duties. See how his "light shineth before men, that they may see his good works." "We commend ourselves," saith he, "to every man's conscience in the sight of God." And again, "For we provide things honest, not only in the Sight of God, but also in the sight of men." And again, "Please all men in all things, even as I please all men in all things." See, on the other hand, how he takes heed, that "he do not his righteousness before men to be seen of them." "Let every man," saith he, "prove his own work, and then shall he have glorying in himself, and not in another." And again, "For our glorying is this, the testimony of our conscience." And that, than which nothing is plainer; "If," saith he, "I yet pleased men, I should not be the servant of Christ."

The very words of the Gospel carry with them their own explanation; nor do they shut the mouths of those who hunger, seeing they feed the hearts of them that knock. The intention of a man's heart, its direction and its aim, is what is to be regarded. For if he who wishes his good works to be seen of men, sets before men his own glory and advantage, and seeks for this in the sight of men, he does not fulfil either of those precepts which the Lord has given as touching this matter; because he has at once looked to "doing his righteousness before men to be seen of them;" and his light has not so shined before men that they should see his good works, and glorify his Father Which is in heaven. It was himself he wished to be glorified, not God; he sought his own advantage, and loved not the Lord's Will. Of such the Apostle says, "For all seek their own, not the things which are Jesus Christ's." Accordingly the sentence was not finished at the words, "Let your light so shine before men, that they may see your good works;" but there was immediately subjoined why this was to be done; "that they may glorify your Father Which is in heaven;" that when a man who does good works is seen of men, he may have only the intention of the good work in his own conscience, but may have no intention of being known, save for the praise of God, for their advantage-sake to whom he is thus made known; for to them this advantage comes, that God Who has given this power to man begins to be well-pleasing to them; and so they do not despair, but that the same power might be vouchsafed to themselves also if they would. And so He did not conclude the other precept, "Take heed that ye do not your righteousness before men," otherwise than in the words, "to be seen of them;" nor did He add in this case, "that they may glorify your Father Which is in heaven," but rather, "otherwise ye have no reward of your Father Which is in heaven." For by this He shews us, that they who are such as He will not have His faithful ones to be, seek a reward in this very thing, that they are seen of men, that it is in this they place their good, in this that they delight the vanity of their heart, in this is their emptiness, and inflation, their swelling and wasting away. For why was it not sufficient to say, "Take heed that ye do not your righteousness before men," but that He added, "that ye may be seen of them," except because there are some who do their righteousness "before men;" not that they may be seen of them, but that the works themselves may be seen; and the Father which is in heaven, Who hath vouchsafed to endow with these gifts the ungodly whom He had justified, may be glorified.

They who are such, neither do they account their righteousness as their own, but His, by the faith of Whom they live; whence also the Apostle says, "that I may win Christ and be found in Him, not having mine own righteousness which is of the law, but that which is of the faith of Christ, the righteousness which is of God by faith;" and in another place,

"That we may be the righteousness of God in Him." Whence also he finds fault with the Jews in these words, "Being ignorant of God's righteousness, and wishing to establish their own righteousness, they have not submitted themselves to the righteousness of God." Whosoever then wish their good works to be so seen of men, that He may be glorified from Whom they have received those things which are seen in them, and that thereby those very persons who see them, may through the dutifulness of faith be provoked to imitate the good, their light shines truly before men, because there beams forth from them the light of charity; theirs is no mere empty fume of pride; and in the very act they take precautions, that they do not their righteousness before men to be seen of them, in that they do not reckon that righteousness as their own, nor do they therefore do it that they may be seen; but that He may be made known, Who is praised in them that are justified, that so He may bring to pass in him that praises that which is praised in others, that is, that He may make him that praises to be himself the object of praise. Observe the Apostle too, how that when he had said, "Please all men in all things, as I also please all men in all things;" he did not stop there, as if he had placed in that, namely, the pleasing men, the end of his intention; for else he would have said falsely, "If I yet pleased men, I should not be the servant of Christ," but he subjoined immediately why it was that he pleased men; "Not seeking," saith he, "mine own profit, but the profit of many, that they may be saved." So that he at once did not please men for his own profit, lest he should not be "the servant of Christ;" and he did please men for their salvation's sake, that he might be a faithful minister of Christ; because for him his own conscience in the Sight of God was enough, and from him there shined forth in the sight of men something which they might imitate.

Sermons on the New Test. IV.

First Sunday in Lent.

REJOICING ALWAYS. S. CHRYSOSTOM.

THERE is nothing whatever that will be able to afflict one who is well ordered in mind, and careful about his own soul; but he will enjoy a pure and continual pleasure. And this ye have heard from St. Paul, who exhorts us, saying, "Rejoice in the Lord always, and again I say, Rejoice." (Phil. iv. 4.)

We know that to many this saying seems impossible. "For how is it possible," says some one, "that he who is but a man, can continually rejoice? To rejoice is no hard matter, but to rejoice continually, this seems to me to be impossible." For many are the causes of sadness which surround us on all sides. A man has lost either a son, or a wife, or a beloved friend, more necessary to him than all kindred, or he has to sustain the loss of wealth; or he has fallen into sickness; or he has to bear some other change of fortune; or to grieve for contemptuous treatment which he did not deserve; or famine, or pestilence, or some intolerable exaction, or circumstances in his family trouble him; nay, there is no saying how many circumstances of a public or private nature are accustomed to occasion us grief. How then, he may say, is it possible to rejoice always? Yea, O man, it is possible, and if it were not so, Paul would not have given the exhortation.

All mankind are universally desirous of pleasure and gladness, but all are not able to attain it, since they know not the way which leads to it; but many suppose that the source of it is in being rich. But if this were its source, no one possessed of wealth would ever be sad. But in fact many of the rich think life not worth living, and would infinitely prefer death when they meet with any hardship; and of all men are most exposed to excessive sadness. For you should not look to their tables, or their flatterers, but to the trouble that comes of such things; the tumults, the calumnies, the dangers, and the alarms, and what is far worse, that they meet these reverses unpractised, and know not how to bear with fortitude what befalls them; whence it happens that calamities do not appear to them such as they are in their own nature, but even things which are really light come to seem intolerable; whereas, with regard to the poor, the contrary takes place; things that are irremediable, seem easy to be borne, since they are familiar with many such.

Others again suppose, that to enjoy good health is the source of pleasure. But it is not so. For many of those who enjoy good health have a thousand times wished themselves dead, not being able to bear the injuries that have befallen them. Others again affirm, that to enjoy glory, and to have attained to power, and to administer the highest offices, and to be flattered by multitudes, is productive of unceasing gladness. But neither is this the case. And why do I speak of other offices of power? for although we were to mount up to royalty itself, we should find it encompassed with a diversity of troubles, and having so many necessary causes the more of sadness, in proportion as it is surrounded with a greater weight of affairs. And kings have of necessity as many causes of sadness as there are waves on the ocean. But if monarchy is unable to render life devoid of grief, then what else can possibly achieve this? Nothing indeed of this life; but this saying of Paul alone, brief and simple as it is, will open to us this very treasure.

For many words are not needed, nor a long round of argument; if we only consider his expression, we shall find the way that leads to it. He does not simply say, "Rejoice always;" but he adds the cause of the continual pleasure, saying, "Rejoice in the Lord always." He who rejoices in the Lord, cannot be deprived of the pleasure by anything that may happen. For all other things in which we rejoice are mutable, liable to become fugitive, and subject to variation. And not only does this grievous circumstance attend them, but moreover while they remain they do not afford us a pleasure sufficient to repel and conceal the sadness that comes upon us from other quarters. But the fear of God contains both these requisites. It is firm and immoveable, and sheds so much gladness that we can admit no sense of other evils. For the man who fears God as he ought, and trusts in Him, gathers from the very root of pleasure, and has possession of the whole fountain of joy. And as a spark falling upon a wide ocean quickly disappears, so whatever events happen to the man who fears God, these, falling as it were upon an immense ocean of joy, are quenched and destroyed! This indeed is most to be wondered at, that whilst things which minister sadness are present, the man should remain joyful. For if there was nothing to produce grief, it would be no great matter to him that he was able continually to rejoice; but that at a time when he is urged to sadness by the pressure of many things, he is superior to all these, this is truly a matter of astonishment. And as no one would have wondered that the three Children were not burnt, if they had remained far off from the furnace of Babylon, (for the circumstance that astonished all was, that having been so long in such close contact with the fire, they left it more free from hurt, than those who had not been in contact with it;) so also we are able to say of the saints, that if no temptation had fastened itself upon them, we should not have wondered at their continual rejoicing. But the point worthy of admiration, and which surpasses human nature, is this, that being encircled on all sides with innumerable waves, they are placed in a far better condition than those who enjoy an entire calm!

It is evident then, that there is no possibility of finding any situation in life, encircled with continual gladness from the things without. But I will endeavour also to prove this point, that the believer is one who cannot possibly be deprived of the enjoyment of a continual pleasure; to the end that ye may not only learn, but aspire after, this condition of life, which is devoid of grief. For suppose a man having nothing for which to condemn himself, but cherishing a good conscience, and panting after the future state, and the fulfilment of those good hopes; what, I ask, will be able to throw such a person into sadness? Does not death seem the most insupportable of all things? Yet the expectation of this is so far from grieving him, that it makes him the more joyful; for he knows that the arrival of death is a release from labour, and a speeding towards the crowns and rewards laid up for those who have contended in the race of piety and virtue. But is it the untimely end of his children? Nay, he will also bear this nobly, and will take up the words of Job, "The Lord gave, the Lord hath taken away; as it seemed good unto the Lord, so it came to pass. Blessed be the Name of the Lord for ever." (Job i. 21.) But if death and the loss of children cannot grieve, much less can the loss of money, or dishonour, or reproaches, or false accusations, at any time affect a soul so great and noble; no, nor anguish of body, since the apostles were scourged, and considered their very scourgings as a subject of additional pleasure. "And they departed from the council, rejoicing that they were counted worthy to suffer shame for the Name of Christ." Did any person insult and revile such an one? Well, he was taught by Christ to rejoice in these revilings. "Rejoice," saith He, "and be exceeding glad, when they shall say all manner of evil against you falsely for My Sake: for great is your reward in Heaven." But suppose a man hath fallen into disease? He hath, however, heard another admonishing and saying, "In disease and poverty trust thou in Him; for as gold is tried in the fire, so are acceptable men in the furnace of humiliation." (Ecclus. ii. 4, 5.)

"What then," says some one, "used not the saints to be in sadness? Do you not hear Paul saying, 'I have great heaviness and continual sorrow in my heart?'" This indeed is the thing to wonder at, that sorrow brought a gain, and a pleasure that resulted from the gain, for as the scourge did not minister to them anguish, but gladness; so also again, the sorrow ministered to them those great crowns. And this is the paradox, that not only the sadness of the world, but also its joy, contains extreme loss; but with regard to spiritual things, it is entirely the opposite, and not the joy only, but the sadness too contains a rich treasure of good things.

If thou hast grieved on account of sin, thou hast blotted it out, and hast reaped the greatest pleasure. If thou hast grieved for thy brethren who have fallen, thou hast both encouraged and comforted thyself, and hast also restored them ; and even if thou wert not to profit them, thou hast an abundant recompence. So that if any one entertains a godly sorrow, he will thence reap a great advantage.

Since therefore those who are in tribulation among us are more blessed than those who are free from it without; and those who are sad are more blessed than those in pleasure, what further source of tribulation shall we have? On this account we should call no man happy, save him only who lives according to God. These only the Scripture terms blessed, for " Blessed," it is said, " is the man who hath not walked in the counsel of the ungodly. Blessed is he whom Thou chastenest, and teachest him out of Thy Law. Blessed are the undefiled in the way. Blessed are all they who trust in Him. Blessed is the people whose God is the Lord. Blessed is he whom his soul condemneth not. Blessed is the man that feareth the Lord." And again, Christ speaks thus: " Blessed are they that mourn: blessed are the humble; blessed are the meek; blessed are the peacemakers; blessed are they who are persecuted for righteousness' sake." Seest thou how the divine laws everywhere pronounce blessed none of the rich, or of the well born, or of the possessors of glory, but those who have gotten hold of virtue. For what is required of us is, that in every thing we do or suffer, the fear of God should be the foundation; and if you implant this as the root, not merely will ease, and honour, and glory and attention, germinate fruits that shall be pleasurable to thee; but hostilities also, and calumnies, and contempt and disgrace, and torments, and all things without exception. And just as the roots of trees are bitter, and yet they produce our sweetest fruits; so verily godly sorrow will bring us an abundant pleasure. They know, who have often prayed with anguish, and shed tears, what gladness they have reaped; how they purged the conscience; how they rose up with favourable hopes. For it is not the nature of the things, but our disposition, which usually makes us sad or joyful. If then we can render the latter such as it ought to be, we shall have a pledge for all gladness.

If then thou desirest joy, seek not after riches, nor bodily health, nor glory, nor power, nor luxury, nor sumptuous tables, nor vestures of silk, nor choice lands, nor houses splendid and conspicuous, nor any other thing of that sort; but pursue that wisdom which is according to God, and take hold of virtue; and then nought of the things which are present, or which are expected, will be able to sadden thee, verily the things that make others sad will prove to thee an accession of pleasure.

De Stat. XVIII. 3—12.

First Monday in Lent.

ESTEEMING GOD MORE THAN MAN.
S. Chrysostom.

. . . "Not only angels are looking on at us, but He that presides over all the spectacle."

Let us not then desire any others to applaud us. For this is to insult Him; hastening by Him, as if insufficient to admire us, we make the best of our way to our fellow-servants. For just as they who contend in a small theatre, seek a large one, as if this were insufficient for their display; so also do they, who, contending in the Sight of God, afterwards seek the applause of men; losing the greater praise and eager for the less, they draw upon themselves severe punishment. What but this hath turned everything upside down? This puts the whole world into confusion, that we do all things with an eye to men, and even for our good things we esteem it nothing to have God as an Admirer, but seek the approbation which cometh from our fellow-servants; and for the contrary things again, despising Him, we fear men. And yet surely they shall stand with us before that tribunal doing us no good. But God, Whom we despise now, shall Himself pass the sentence upon us.

But yet though we know these things, we still gape after men, which is the first of sins. Thus, were a man looking on, no one would choose to be guilty of iniquity, the tyranny of his passion is conquered by his reverence for men. But in God's Sight, men have dared and still dare to do very many dreadful things. In the sight of men we fear, but in God's Sight, we fear no longer. From hence in fact, all the world's evils have originated; because in things so bad, we reverence not God but men.

On this account you see, both things which are truly good, not accounted such by the generality, because objects of our aversion: men not investigating the nature of the things, but having respect unto the opinion of the many; and again in the case of evil things, acting on this same principle. Certain things therefore are not really good, but seeming fair unto the many, we pursue as good, through the same habit. So that on either side we go to destruction.

Perhaps some may find this remark somewhat obscure; wherefore we must express it more clearly. When we commit sin, we fear men more than God. When therefore we have thus subjected ourselves unto them, and made them lords over us, there are many other things also, which seem unto these our lords to be evil, not being such; these also we flee for our part in like manner. For instance: to live in poverty many account disgraceful; and we flee poverty, not because it is disgraceful or because we are so persuaded, but because our masters count it disgraceful; and we fear them. Again, to be unhonoured, and contemptible, and void of all authority, seems likewise unto the most part a matter of shame and great vileness. This again we flee; not condemning the thing itself, but because of the sentence of our masters.

Again on the contrary side also we undergo the same mischief. As wealth is counted a good thing, and pride and pomps, and to be conspicuous: accordingly this again we pursue, not either in this case from considering the nature of the thing as good, but persuaded by the opinion of our masters. For the people is our master; and the great mob is a savage master, and a severe tyrant: not so much as a command being needed in order to make us listen to him, it is enough that we just know what he wills, and without a command we submit: so great good will do we bear towards him. Again, God threatening and admonishing, day by day, is not heard; but the common people, full of disorders. made up of all manner of dregs, has no occasion for one word of command; enough for it only to signify with what it is well pleased, and in all things we obey immediately.

"But how," says some one, "is a man to flee from these masters?" By getting a mind greater than theirs; by looking into the nature of things; by condemning the voice of the multitude; before all, by training himself in things really disgraceful to fear not men, but the Unsleeping Eye; and again in all good things, to seek the crowns which come from Him. For thus neither in the other sort of things shall we be able to tolerate them. For whoso when he doth right, judges them unworthy to know his good deeds, and contents himself with the suffrage of God; neither will he take account of them in matters of the contrary sort.

"And how can this be?" You will say, Consider what man is, what God, Whom thou desertest, and unto Whom thou fliest for refuge; and thou wilt soon be right altogether. Man lieth under the same sin as thyself, and the same condemnation, and the same punishment. "Man is like to vanity," and hath not true judgment, and needs the correction from above. "Man is dust and ashes," and if he bestow praise, he will often bestow it at random, or out of favour or ill will. And if he calumniate and accuse, this again will he do out of the same kind of purpose. But God doeth not so: rather irreprovable is His sentence, and pure His judgment. Wherefore we must always flee to Him for refuge, and not for these reasons alone, but because He both made, and more than all spares thee, and loves thee better than thou dost thyself.

Why then, neglecting to have so awful an approver, betake we ourselves unto man, who is nothing, all rashness, all at random? Doth he call thee wicked and polluted when thou art not so? So much the more do thou pity him, and weep because he is corrupt: and despise his opinion, because the eyes of his understanding are darkened. For even the apostles were thus evil reported of, and they laughed to scorn their calumniators. But doth he call thee good or kind? If such indeed thou art, yet be not at all puffed up by the opinion; but if thou art not

D

such, despise it the more, and esteem the thing to be mockery.

What can it be but the extreme of folly to seek earnestly the praise of men, so corrupt in their ideas, men whose conduct is all at random, when we ought always to resort to the Unsleeping Eye, and look to His sentence in all that we do and speak? For these, even if they approve, will have no power to profit us. But He, should He accept our doings, will both here make us glorious, and in the future day will impart to us of the unspeakable good things, which may it be the lot of us all to obtain, through the Grace and Loving-kindness of our Lord Jesus Christ, to Whom with the Father and the Holy Spirit be glory, honour, power, now and always, and unto everlasting ages. Amen.

In 1 Cor. Hom. xii.

First Tuesday in Lent.

GOOD USE OF TIME. S. CHRYSOSTOM.

To be supported by continual hard work is a sort of asceticism. The souls of such men are clearer and their minds better strung. For the man who has nothing to do is apter to say many things at random, and do many things at random; and he is busy all day long about nothing, a huge lethargy taking him up entirely. But he that is employed will not lightly entertain in himself any thing useless, in deeds, in words, or in thoughts; for his whole soul is altogether intent upon his laborious way of livelihood. Let us not therefore despise those who support themselves by the labour of their own hands; but let us rather call them happy on this account. For tell me, what thanks are due unto thee, when, after having received thy portion from thy father, thou goest not on in any calling, but lavishing away the whole of it at random? Knowest thou not that we shall not all have to render the same account, but those who have enjoyed greater licence here, a more exact one; those who were afflicted with labour, or poverty, or any thing else of this kind, one not so severe? And this is plain from Lazarus and the rich man. For as thou for neglecting the right use of thy leisure art justly accused; so the poor man, who having full employment hath spent his remnant of time upon right objects, great will be the crowns which he shall receive. But dost thou urge that a soldier's duties should at least excuse thee; and dost thou charge them with thy want of leisure? The excuse cannot be founded in reason. For Cornelius was a centurion, yet in no way did the soldier's belt impair his strict rule of life. But thou, when thou art keeping holiday with idle companions, and making entire waste of thy life, never thinkest of excusing thyself by the necessity of military service, or the fear of rulers, but when it is the Church to which we call you, then occur these endless impediments.

And what wilt thou say in that day, when thou seest the flame, and the rivers of fire, and the chains never to be broken, and shalt hear the gnashing of teeth? Who shall stand up for thee in that day, when thou shalt see him that hath laboured with his own hands and hath lived uprightly, enjoying all glory; but thyself, who art now in silken robes and steaming with perfumes, in incurable woe? What good will thy wealth and superfluity do thee? And the poor man, what harm will his poverty do him?

Therefore that we may not suffer then, let us fear what is said now, and let all our time of occupation be spent in employment on things which are really indispensable. For so, having propitiated God in regard of our past sins, and adding good deeds for the future, we shall be able to attain unto the kingdom of heaven: through the favour and loving-kindness of God.

In 1 Cor. Hom. v.

Second Wednesday in Lent.

ALMSGIVING. S. AUGUSTINE.

"Go, sell all that thou hast, and give to the poor."

Our God hath not, as unbelieving covetous men suppose, wished us to lose what we have: if what hath been enjoined us be properly understood, and piously believed, and devoutly received, He hath not enjoined us to lose, but rather shewn a place where we may lay up. For no man can help thinking of his treasure, and following his riches in a kind of journeying of the heart. If then they are buried in the earth, his heart will seek the lowest earth; but if they are reserved in heaven, his heart will be above. If Christians therefore have the will to do what they know, that they also make open profession of[1], if they have the will to "lift up the heart" above, let them lay up there, what they love; and though yet in the flesh on earth, let them dwell with Christ in heart; and as her Head went before the Church, so let the heart of the Christian go before him. As the members are to go where Christ the Head hath gone before, so shall each man at his rising again go where his heart hath now gone before. Let us go hence then by that part of us which we may; our whole man will follow whither one part of us is gone before. Our earthly house must fall to ruin, our heavenly house is eternal. Let us move our goods beforehand, whither we are ourselves getting ready to come.

We have just heard a certain rich man seeking counsel from the Good Master as to the means of obtaining eternal life. Great was the thing he loved, and of little value was that he was unwilling

---

[1] S. Augustine here alludes to the Sursum Corda of the communicants. "Lift up your hearts." "We lift them up unto the Lord."

to renounce. And so in perverseness of heart, on hearing Him Whom he had but now called " Good Master," through the overpowering love of what was valueless, he lost the possession of what was of great price. If he had not wished to obtain eternal life, he would not have asked counsel how to obtain it. How is it then, brethren, that he rejected the words of Him Whom he had called Good Master, drawn out for him as they were from the doctrine of the faith? What? Is He a good Master before He teacheth, and when He hath taught a bad one? He did not hear what he wished, but he did hear what was proper for him; he had come with longing, but he went away in sadness. What if He had told him, " Lose what thou hast," when he went away sad because it was said, " Keep what thou hast securely?" " Go," saith He, " sell all that thou hast and give to the poor." Art thou afraid, it may be, lest thou shouldest lose it? See what follows; "and thou shalt have treasure in heaven." Before now, it may be, thou hast set some young slave to guard thy treasures; thy God will be the Guardian of thy gold. He Who gave them on earth will Himself keep them in heaven. Perhaps he would not have hesitated to commit what he had to Christ, and was only sad because it was told him, " give to the poor;" as though he would say in his heart, " Hadst Thou said, Give it to Me, I will keep it in heaven for thee; I would not hesitate to give it to my Lord, the Good Master; but now Thou hast said, Give to the poor."

Let no one fear to lay out upon the poor, let no

ALMSGIVING. 39

one think that he is the receiver whose hand he sees. He receives it Who bade thee give it. And this I say not out of mine own heart, or by any human conjecture; hear Him Himself Who at once exhorteth thee, and giveth thee a title of security. " I was an hungred," saith He, "and ye gave Me meat." And when after the enumeration of all their kind offices they answered, "When saw we Thee an hungred?" He answered, "Inasmuch as ye have done it unto one of the least of these of Mine, ye have done it unto Me." It is the poor man who begs, but He that is Rich receives. Thou givest it to one who will make away with it, He receiveth it Who will restore it. Nor will He restore only what He receiveth; He is pleased to borrow upon interest, He promiseth more than thou hast given. Give the rein now to thy avarice, imagine thyself an usurer. If thou wert an usurer indeed, thou wouldst be rebuked by the Church, confuted by the Word of God, all thy brethren would execrate thee, as a cruel man, desiring to wring gain from others' tears. But now be a usurer, no one will hinder thee. Thou art willing to lend to a poor man, who whenever he may repay thee will do it with grief, but lend now to a debtor who is well able to pay, and who even exhorteth thee to receive what He promiseth.

Give to God, and press God for payment. Yea rather give to God and thou wilt be pressed to receive payment. On earth indeed thou hadst to seek thy debtor; and he sought too, but only to find where he might hide himself from thy face. Thou hadst gone to the judge and said, "Bid that my debtor be summoned;" and he on hearing this gets away, and cares not even to wish thee well, though to him perhaps in his need thou hadst given wealth by thy loan. Thou hast One then on whom thou mayest well lay out thy money. Give to Christ; He will of His own accord press thee to receive, whilst thou wilt even wonder that He hath received aught of thee. For to them who are placed on His Right Hand He will first say, "Come, ye blessed of My Father." Come whither? "Receive the kingdom prepared for you from the foundation of the world." For what? "For I was an hungred, and ye gave Me meat; I was thirsty, and ye gave Me drink; I was a stranger, and ye took Me in; naked, and ye clothed Me; I was sick and in prison, and ye visited Me." And they will say, "Lord, when saw we Thee?" What doth this mean? The debtor presses to pay, and the creditors make excuses. But the trusty debtor will not let them suffer loss thereby. "Do ye hesitate to receive? I have received, and are ye ignorant of it?" And he makes answer how He has received; "Inasmuch as ye have done it unto one of the least of these of Mine, ye have done it unto Me." I received it not by Myself, but by Mine; what was given to them, came to Me; be secure, ye have not lost it. Ye look to those who were little able to pay on earth, ye have One Who is well able to pay in heaven. "I," He saith, "have received, and I will repay."

And what have I received, and what do I repay?

"I was an hungred," He saith, "and ye gave Me meat;" I received earth, I will give heaven; I received temporal things, I will restore eternal; I received bread, I will give life. Yea, we may even say thus, I have received bread, I will give Bread; I have received drink, I will give Drink; I have received house-room, I will give a House; I was visited in sickness, I will give Health; I was visited in prison, I will give Liberty. The bread which ye gave to My poor is consumed; the Bread which I will give both recruiteth the failing and doth not itself fail. May He then give us Bread, He Who is the Living Bread which came down from heaven. When He shall give Bread, He will give Himself. For what didst thou intend when thou didst lend on usury? To give money, and to receive money, but to give a smaller sum, and to receive a larger. "I," saith God, " will give thee an exchange for the better for all that thou hast given Me. For if thou wert to give a pound of silver, and receive a pound of gold, with how great joy wouldest thou be possessed? What proportion is there between silver and gold! Much more then, what proportion is there between earth and heaven! And thy silver and gold thou wert to leave here below; whereas thou wilt not abide thyself for ever here. And I will give thee something else, and I will give thee something more, and I will give thee something better, I will give thee even that which will last for ever."

Homil. on the New Test., xxxvi.

Second Thursday in Lent.

DANGER OF EVIL WORDS. S. Chrysostom.

"Whosoever shall say, Thou fool, shall be in danger of hell fire."

To many this commandment hath appeared grievous and galling, if for a mere word we are really to pay so great a penalty. And some even say that it was spoken rather hyperbolically. But I fear lest, when we have deceived ourselves with words here, we may in deeds there suffer that extreme punishment. For wherefore, tell me, doth the commandment seem over-burdensome? Knowest thou not that most punishments and most sins have their beginnings from words? Yea, for by words are blasphemies, and denials are by words, and revilings and reproaches, and perjuries, and bearing false witness. Regard not then its being a mere word, but whether it have not much danger, this do thou enquire. Art thou ignorant that in the season of enmity, when wrath is inflamed, and the soul kindled, even the least thing appears great, and what is not very reproachful is counted intolerable? And often these little things have given birth even to murder, and overthrown whole cities. For just as where friendship is, even grievous things are light, so where enmity lies beneath, very trifles appear intolerable, and however simply a word be spoken, it is surmised to have been spoken with an evil meaning. And as in fire: if there be but a small spark, though thousands of planks lie by, it doth not easily lay hold of them; but if the flame have waxed strong and high, it readily seizes not planks only, but stones, and all materials that fall in its way; and by what things it is usually quenched, by the same it is kindled the more; (for some say that at such a time not only wood and tow, and the other combustibles, but even water darted forth upon it doth but fan its power the more;) whatever any one may say, becomes food in a moment for this evil conflagration. All which kind of evils Christ checking beforehand, had condemned first him that is angry without a cause to the judgment, then him that saith Raca to the council. But as yet these are no great things, for the punishments are here. Therefore for him who calleth fool He hath added the fire of hell, now for the first time (in His sermon on the mount) mentioning the name of hell. For having before discoursed much of the Kingdom, not until then did He mention this: implying that the former cometh of His own Love and indulgence towards man, this latter of our negligence.

And see how He proceeds by little and little in His punishments, all but excusing Himself unto thee, and signifying that His desire indeed is to threaten nothing of the kind, but that we drag Him on to such denunciations. For observe; "I bade thee," saith He, "not be angry for nought, because thou art in danger of the judgment. Thou hast despised the former commandment: see what anger hath produced; it hath led thee on straightway to insult, for thou hast called thy brother Raca. Again, I set another punishment, the council. If thou overlook even this, and proceed to that which is more grievous, I visit thee no longer with these finite punishments, but with the undying penalty of hell, lest after this thou shouldest break forth even to murder." For there is nothing, nothing in the world, more intolerable than insolence, it is what hath very great power to sting a man's soul. But when the word too which is spoken is in itself more wounding than the insolence, the blaze becomes twice as great. Think it not then a light thing to call another fool. For when of that which separates us from the brutes, and by which especially we are human beings, namely, the mind and the understanding, when of this thou hast robbed thy brother, thou hast deprived him of all his nobleness.

Let us not then regard the words merely, but realizing the things themselves, and his feeling, let us consider how great a wound is made by this word, and unto how much evil it proceeds. For this cause Paul likewise cast out of the kingdom not only the adulterous and effeminate, but the revilers also. (1 Cor. vi. 9, 10.) And with great reason, for the insolent man mars all the beauty of charity, and casts upon his neighbour unnumbered ills, and works everlasting enmities, and tears asunder the members of Christ, and is daily driving away that peace which God so desires: giving much vantage-ground unto the devil by his injurious ways, and making him the stronger. Therefore Christ Himself, cutting out the sinews of the devil's power, brought in this law.

For indeed He makes much account of love: this being above all things the mother of every good, and the badge of His disciples, and the bond which holds together our whole condition. With reason therefore doth He remove with great earnestness the roots and the sources of that hatred which utterly spoils it.

Think not therefore that these sayings are in any wise hyperbolical, but consider the good done by them, and admire the mildness of these laws. For there is nothing for which God takes so much pains as this; that we should be united and knit together one with another. Therefore both in His Own Person, and by His disciples, as well those in the Old, as in the New Testament, He makes so much account of this commandment; and is a severe avenger and punisher of those who despise the duty. For in truth nothing so effectually gives entrance and root to all wickedness, as the taking away of love. Wherefore He also said, "When iniquity abounds, the love of many shall wax cold." Thus Cain became his brother's murderer; thus Esau; thus Joseph's brethren; thus our unnumbered crimes have come revelling in, this bond being dissevered. You see why He Himself also roots out whatever things injure this, on every side, with great exactness.

Homil. on S. Matt. xvi.

Second Friday in Lent.

PRAYER. S. AUGUSTINE.

Do ye think, brethren, that God doth not know what is needful for you? He knoweth and preventeth our desires, Who knoweth our want. And so when He taught His disciples to pray, and warned them not to use many words in prayer, He saith, "Use not many words: for your Father knoweth what things ye have need of before ye ask Him." If our Father knoweth what things we have need of before we ask Him, why do we use even few words? What is the use of prayer at all, if our Father knoweth already "what things we have need of?" He saith to one, Do not make thy prayer to me at great length: for I know what is needful for thee. If so, Lord, why should I so much as pray at all? Thou wouldest not that I should use long prayers, yea rather, Thou dost even bid me to use near none at all. And then what meaneth that precept in another place? For He Who saith, "Use not many words in prayer," saith in another place, "Ask, and it shall be given you." And that thou mightest not think that this first precept to ask was cursorily given, He added, "Seek, and ye shall find." And that thou mightest not think that this too was given cursorily, see what He added further, see with what He finished: "Knock, and it shall be opened unto you;" see what He added! He would have thee ask that thou mayest receive, and seek that thou mayest find, and knock that thou mayest enter in. Seeing then that our Father knoweth already what is needful for us, how and why do we ask? why seek? why knock? why weary ourselves in asking, and seeking, and knocking, to instruct Him Who knoweth already? And in another place the words of the Lord are, "Men ought always to pray, and not to faint." If men "ought always to pray," how doth He say, "Use not many words?" How can I always pray, if I so quickly make an end? Here thou biddest me finish quickly; there always to pray and not to faint; what doth this mean? Now that thou mayest understand this, "ask, seek, knock." For for this cause it is closed, not to shut thee out, but to exercise thee. Therefore, brethren, ought we to exhort to prayer both ourselves and you. For other hope have we none amid the manifold evils of this present world, than to knock in prayer, to believe and to maintain the belief firm in the heart, that thy Father only doth not give thee what He knoweth is not expedient for thee. For thou knowest what thou dost desire; He knoweth what is good for thee. Imagine thyself under a physician, and in weak health, as is the very truth; for all this life of ours is a weakness; and a long life is nothing else but a prolonged weakness. Imagine thyself to be sick under the physician's hand. Thou hast a desire to ask thy physician leave to drink a draught of fresh wine.

Thou art not prohibited from asking, for it may chance to do thee no harm, or even good to receive it. Do not then hesitate to ask; ask, hesitate not; but if thou receive not, do not take it to heart. Now if thou wouldest act thus in the hands of a man, the physician of the body, how much more in the Hands of God, Who is the Physician, the Creator, and Restorer, both of thy body and soul?

Wherefore see how the Lord exhorted His disciples to prayer, when He said, "Ye could not cast out this devil because of your unbelief." For then exhorting them to prayer He ended thus; "This kind is not cast out but by prayer and fasting." If a man must pray to cast out devils from another, how much more to cast out his own covetousness, how much more to cast out his own drunkenness? his own luxuriousness? his own uncleanness? How many things in a man are there, which if they are persevered in, allow of no admission into the kingdom of Heaven? Consider, brethren, how a physician is intreated for the preservation of temporal health; how, if any one is desperately ill, is he ashamed or slow to throw himself at a man's feet? to bathe in tears the footsteps of any very able chief physician? And what if the physician say to him, "Thou canst not else be cured, except I bind thee, and use the fire and knife?" He will answer, "Do what thou wilt, only cure me." With what eagerness does he long for the health of a few days, fleeting as a vapour, that for it he is content to be bound, and submit to the fire and knife, and to be watched, that he neither eat nor drink what or when he pleases! All this he will endure that he may die a little later; and yet he will not endure ever so little that he may never die. If God, Who is the heavenly Physician over us, saith to thee, Wilt thou be cured? what wouldest thou say but Yes? Or it may be thou wouldest not say so, because thou fanciest thyself to be in health, that is, because thou art more grievously sick.

Let us then pray, and rely on God: let us live as He enjoineth; and when we totter in this life, let us call upon Him as the disciples called, saying, "Lord, increase our faith." Peter both put his trust in Him, and tottered; but notwithstanding he was not disregarded and left to sink, but was lifted up and raised. For his trust whence was it? Not from any thing of his own, but from what was the Lord's. How? "Lord, if it be Thou, bid me come unto Thee on the water." For I know that if it be Thou, Thou biddest and it is done. "And He saith, Come." Peter went down at His bidding, but in his own weakness he was afraid. Nevertheless when he was afraid, he cried out, "Lord, save me!" Then the Lord took him by the hand, and said, "O thou of little faith, wherefore didst thou doubt?" He first invited him, He delivered him, as he tottered and stumbled, that it might be fulfilled which was said in the Psalm, "If I said, my foot hath slipped, Thy mercy, O Lord, aided me."

Thus are then two kinds of blessings, temporal and eternal. Temporal blessings are health, substance, honour, friends, a home, children, wife, and the other things of this life in which we are sojourners. Put we up then in the hostelry of this life as strangers passing on, and not as owners intending to remain. But eternal blessings are first, eternal life itself, the incorruption and immortality of body and soul, the society of angels, the heavenly city, glory unfailing, Father and fatherland, the former without death, the latter without a foe. These blessings let us desire with all eagerness, let us ask with all perseverance, not with length of words, but with the witness of groans. (Longing desire prayeth always, though the tongue be silent. If thou art ever longing, thou art ever praying.) When sleepeth prayer? When desire groweth cold. So then let us beg for these eternal blessings with all eager desire, let us seek for those good things with an entire earnestness, let us ask for those good things with all assurance. For those good things do profit him that hath them, they cannot harm him. But those other temporal good things sometimes profit, and sometimes harm. Poverty hath profited many, and wealth hath harmed many; a private life hath profited many, and exalted honour hath harmed many. And again, money hath profited some, honourable distinction hath profited some; profited those who use them well; but from those who use them ill, the not withdrawing them hath harmed them more. And so, brethren, let us ask for those temporal blessings too, but in moderation; being sure that if we do receive them, He giveth them, Who knoweth what is expedient for us. Thou hast asked, and what thou hast asked hath not been given thee? Trust thy Father, Who would give it thee, were it expedient for thee. Lo! judge in this case by thine own self. For such as thy son, who knows not the ways of men, is in regard to thee, such in regard to the Lord art thou thyself, who knowest not the things of God. Lo! thy son cries a whole day before thee, that thou wouldest give him a knife, or a sword; thou dost refuse to give it him, thou wilt not give it, thou disregardest his tears, lest thou shouldest have to bewail his death. Let him cry, and beat himself, or throw himself upon the ground, that thou mayest set him on horseback; thou wilt not do it, because he does not know how to govern the horse, which may throw and kill him. To whom thou refusest a part, thou art reserving the whole. But that he may grow up, and possess the whole in safety, thou givest him not that little thing which is full of peril to him.

And so, brethren, we say, pray as much as ye are able. Evils abound, and God hath willed that evils should abound. Would that evil men did not abound, and then evils would not abound. Bad times! troublesome times! This men are saying. Let our lives be good, and the times are good. We make our times; such as we are, such are the times. But what can we do? We cannot, it may be, convert the mass of men to a good life, but let the few who do give ear live well; let the few who live well endure the many who live ill. They are the corn, they are in the floor; in the floor they can have the chaff with them, they will not have them in the barn. Let them endure what they would not, that they may come to what they would. Wherefore are we sad, and blame we God? Evils abound in the world, in order that the world may not engage our love. Great men, faithful saints, were they who have despised the world with all its attractions; we are not able to despise it, even disfigured as it is. The world is evil, lo it is evil, and yet it is loved as though it were good! But what is this evil world? For the heavens and the earth, and the waters, and the things that are therein, the fish, and birds and trees, are not evil. All these are good: but it is evil men who make this evil world. Yet as we cannot be without evil men, let us, as I have said, whilst we live pour out our groans before the Lord our God, and endure the evils, that we may attain to the things that are good. Let us not find fault with the Master of the household, for He is loving to us. He beareth us, and not we Him. He knoweth how to govern what He hath made; let us do what He hath bidden, and hope for what He hath promised.

Sermons on the New Test., xxx.

Second Saturday in Lent.

ON RICHES. S. CHRYSOSTOM.

"Charge them that are rich in this world that they be not high-minded." (1 Tim. vi. 17.)

When S. Paul says, "that are rich in this world," he makes it manifest that there are others who are rich in the world to come: such as was that Lazarus, poor as to the present life, but rich as to the future; not in gold and silver, and such-like contemptible and transitory store of wealth, but in those unutterable good things which eye hath not seen, nor ear heard, nor hath it entered into the heart of man. For this is true wealth and opulence, when there is good unmixed, and not subject to any change. Not such was the case of the rich man who despised Lazarus, but he became afterwards the poorest of mankind. Yea when he sought to obtain but a drop of water, he was not master even of that, to such extreme poverty was he come. For this reason S. Paul calls them rich " in the present world," to teach thee that along with the present life, worldly wealth is annihilated. It goes no further, neither does it change its place with its migrating possessors, but it often leaves them before their end, which therefore he shews by saying, "Neither trust in uncertain riches;" for nothing is so faithless as wealth; it is a runaway, thankless servant, having no fidelity: and should you throw over him ten thousand chains, he would depart dragging his chains after him. When men endeavour with all eagerness to collect so frail and fleeting a thing, they do not hear what the prophet saith, "Woe unto them who trust in their power, and boast themselves in the multitude of their riches." (Ps. xlix. 6.) Tell me why is this woe denounced? "He heapeth up treasure, and knoweth not for whom he will gather it." (Ps. xxxix. 6.) Forasmuch as the labour is certain, but the enjoyment uncertain.

The rich man is not one who is in possession of much, but one who gives much. Abraham was rich, but he was not covetous, he covered not his roof with gold, but fixing his tent near the oak, he was contented with the shadow of its leaves. Yet so illustrious was his lodging, that angels were not ashamed to tarry with him, for they sought not splendour of abode, but virtue of soul. This man then let us imitate, beloved, and bestow what we have upon the needy. That lodging was rudely prepared, but it was more illustrious than the halls of kings. No king has ever entertained angels; but he, dwelling under that oak, and having but pitched a tent, was thought worthy of that honour: not receiving the honour on account of the meanness of his dwelling, but enjoying that benefit on account of the magnificence of his soul and the wealth therein deposited.

Let us too then, adorn not our houses, but our

souls in preference to the house. For is it not disgraceful to clothe our walls with marble, vainly and to no end, and to see Christ going about naked? What does thy house profit thee, O man! For wilt thou take it with thee when thou departest? This thou canst not take with thee when thou departest; but thy soul, when thou departest, thou shalt assuredly take with thee.

We build houses that we may have an habitation, not that we may make an ambitious display. What is byond our wants is superfluous and useless. Put on a sandal which is larger than your foot, you will not endure it; for it is an hindrance to the step. Thus also a house larger than necessity require, is an impediment to your progress towards heavn. Do you wish to build large and splendid houses? I forbid it not; but let it not be upon the eartl! Build thyself tabernacles in heaven, tabernacles that shall never be dissolved! Why art thou mad about fleeting things, and things that must be left here? Nothing is more fallacious than wealth. To-day it is for thee, to-morrow it is against thee.

And these things I say, not because riches are a sin: although there be sin in not distributing them to the poor, and in the wrong use of them. For God made nothing evil, but all things very good; so that riches too are good; i. e. if they do not master their owners; if the wants of our neighbours be done away by them. For neither is that light good which instead of dissipating darkness rather makes it intense; nor should I call that wealth, which instead of doing away poverty, rather increases it. For the rich man seeks not to take from others but to help others: but he that seeks to receive from others is no longer rich, but is emphatically the poor man. So that it is not riches that are evil, but the needy mind which turns wealth into poverty. There are more wretched than those who ask alms in the narow streets, enduring loss of limb and loathsome bodily ills. I say, clothed in rags as they are, they are not so miserable as some in silks and shining garments. Christ stands ready to receive, and to keep thy deposits for thee; and not to keep only, but also to augment them, and to pay them back with such interest. Out of His Hand no man can forcibly take them away.

Thou art a stranger and a pilgrim with respet to the things here! Thou hast a country which is tine own in the heavens! There deposit all; that bfore the actual enjoyment thou mayest enjoy the recompense here. He who is nourished with good hopes and is confident with regard to the things of futurity, hath here already tasted of the Kingdom. For nothing ordinarily so repairs the soul, and makes a man better, as a good hope of futurity, so that if thou deposit thy wealth there, thou mayest then provide for thy soul with suitable leisure. For they who spend all their endeavours upon the ornamenting of their dwelling, rich as they are in outward things, are careless of that which is within, letting their souls abide desolate and filthy, and full of cobwebs. But if they would be indifferent to exterior things, and earnestly expend all their attention upon the mind, adorning this at all points; then the soul of such men would be a tabernacle for Christ. And having Christ for its inhabitant what could ever be more blessed? Wouldest thou be rich? Have God for thy Friend, and thou shalt be richer than all men! Wouldest thou be rich? Be not high-minded! Let us not be high-minded in reference to riches, or indeed to any other thing; for if even in spiritual things the man who is high-minded is fallen and undone, much more so as to carnal things. Let us be mindful of our nature. Let us recollect our sins. Let us learn what we are, and this will provide a sufficient foundation for complete humility.

God hath made thee rich, why makest thou thyself poor? He hath made thee rich that thou mayest assist the needy; that thou mayest have release of thine own sins, by liberality to others. He hath given thee money, not that thou mayest shut it up for thy destruction, but that thou mayest pour it forth for thy salvation. For this reason also He hath made the possession of riches uncertain and unstable, that by this means He might slack the intensity of thy madness concerning it.

Wherefore let us not consider riches to be a great good; for the great good is, not to possess money, but to possess the fear and reverence of God. Let us flee all worldly and disgraceful wealth, and let us obtain that which is spiritual, and let us seek after the treasures in the heavens. For whoso possess there, they are the rich, they are the wealthy, both here and there enjoying things, even all things. To the end then that we may attain both to the good things here and to those which are there, let us choose the wealth which cannot be removed, that immortal abundance : which may God grant us all to obtain through the Grace and Loving-kindness of our Lord Jesus Christ.

De Stat. Hom. ii., and in Cor. Hom. xiii.

Second Sunday in Lent.

THE HOLY CATHOLIC CHURCH.
S. Cyril Jer.

The faith which we rehearse contains in order the following, "And in One Baptism of repentance for the remission of sins ; and in One Holy Catholic Church." On which though one might say many things, we will speak but briefly. Now it is called Catholic because it is throughout the world, from one end of the earth to the other ; and because it teaches universally and completely one and all the doctrines which ought to come to men's knowledge, concerning things both visible and invisible, heavenly and earthly ; and because it subjugates in order to godliness every class of men, governors and governed, learned and unlearned ; and because it universally treats and heals every sort of sins which are committed by soul or body, and possesses in itself every form of virtue which is named, both in deeds and words, and in every kind of spiritual gifts.

And it is rightly named Church, because it calls forth and assembles together all men, according as the Lord says in Leviticus, " And assemble thou all the congregation to the doors of the tabernacle of witness." And it is to be noted, that the word " assemble " is used for the first time in the Scriptures here, at the time when the Lord puts Aaron into the high priesthood. And in Deuteronomy the Lord says to Moses, " Assemble to Me the people, and I will make them hear My words, that they shall learn to fear Me." And he again mentions the name of the Church, when he says concerning the Tables, " And on them was written according to all the words which the Lord spake with you in the mount out of the midst of the fire in the day of the assembly ;" as if he had said more plainly, in the day in which ye were called and gathered together by God. And the Psalmist says, " I will give Thee thanks in the great assembly; I will praise Thee among much people."

Of old the Psalmist sung, " Bless ye God in the Church, even the Lord, from the fountain of Israel." But since the Jews for their evil designs against the Saviour have been cast away from grace, the Saviour has built out of the Gentiles a second Holy Church, the Church of us Christians, concerning which He said to Peter, " And upon this rock I will build My Church, and the gates of hell shall not prevail against it." And David, prophesying of both, said plainly of the first, which was rejected, "I have hated the Church of the evil doers;" but of the second, which is built up, he says in the same Psalm, "Lord, I have loved the habitation of Thine House;" and immediately afterwards, "In the Churches will I bless the Lord." For now that the one Church in Judea is cast off, the Churches of Christ are increased throughout the world; and of them it is said, "Sing unto the Lord a new song, and His praise in the Church of the Saints." Agreeably to which the Prophet also said to the Jews, "I have no pleasure in you, saith the Lord of Hosts;" and immediately afterwards, "For from the rising of the sun even unto the going down of the same, My Name shall be great among the Gentiles." Concerning this Holy Catholic Church Paul writes to Timothy, "That thou mayest know how thou oughtest to behave thyself in the House of God, which is the Church of the Living God, the pillar and ground of the truth."

But since the word church or assembly is applied to different things, (as also it is written of the multitude in the theatre of the Ephesians, "And when he had thus spoken, he dismissed the assembly," and since one might properly and truly say that there is a "church of the evil doers," I mean the meetings of the heretics, the Marcionists and Manichees, and the rest,) the faith has delivered to thee by way of security the Article, "And in ONE Holy Catholic Church;" that thou mayest avoid their wretched meetings, and ever abide with the Holy Church

Catholic in which thou wast regenerated. And if ever thou art sojourning in any city, enquire not simply where the Lord's house is, (for the sects of the profane also make an attempt to call their own dens houses of the Lord,) nor merely where the Church is, but where is the Catholic Church. For this is the peculiar name of this holy Body, the Mother of us all, which is the Spouse of our Lord Jesus Christ, the Only-begotten Son of God, (for it is written, "As Christ also loved the Church and gave Himself for it," and all the rest,) and is a figure and copy of Jerusalem "above, which is free and the mother of us all;" which before was barren, but now has many children.

For when the first Church was cast off, God in the second, which is the Catholic Church, "hath set first apostles, secondarily prophets, thirdly teachers, after that miracles, then gifts of healings, helps, governments, diversities of tongues," and every sort of virtue; I mean wisdom and understanding, temperance and justice, alms-doing and loving-kindness, and patience unconquerable in persecutions. She, "by the armour of righteousness on the right hand and on the left, by honour and dishonour," in former days amid persecutions and tribulations, crowned the holy martyrs with the varied and blooming chaplets of patience, and now in times of peace by God's grace receives her due honours from princes and nobles, and from every rank and kindred of man. And while the kings of particular nations have bounds set to their dominion, the Holy Church Catholic alone extends her illimitable sovereignty over the whole world; "for God," as it is written, "hath made her border peace." But I should need many more hours for my discourse, would I speak of all things which concern her.

In this Holy Catholic Church receiving instruction and behaving ourselves virtuously, we shall attain the kingdom of heaven, and inherit eternal life; for which also we endure all toils, that we may be made partakers of it from the Lord. For ours is no trifling aim; eternal life is our object of pursuit. Wherefore in the profession of the faith, after the words, "And in the resurrection of the flesh," that is, of the dead, we are taught to believe, "And in the life everlasting," for which, as Christians, we are striving.

The Father is the real and true life; and He through the Son in the Holy Spirit pours forth as from a fountain His heavenly gifts to all; for through His love to man, the blessings of everlasting life are promised without fail even to us men. We must not disbelieve the possibility of this, but having an eye not to our own weakness but to His power, we must believe; "for with God all things are possible." And that this is possible, and that we may look for everlasting life, Daniel declares, "And they that turn many to righteousness as the stars for ever and ever." And Paul says, "And so shall we be ever with the Lord:" now the "being for ever with the Lord" implies life everlasting. But most plainly of all the Saviour Himself says in the Gospel, "And these shall go away into everlasting punishment, but the righteous into life eternal."

And many are the proofs concerning the life everlasting. And when we desire to gain this eternal life, the sacred Scriptures suggest to us the ways of gaining it; of which, because of the length, the texts which we set before you shall be few, the rest being left to the search of the diligent. They declare at one time that it is by faith, for it is written, "He that believeth on the Son hath everlasting life," &c.: and again, He says Himself, "Verily, verily, I say unto you, He that heareth My words, and believeth on Him that sent Me, hath everlasting life," &c. At another time it is by the preaching of the Gospel, for He says that "He that reapeth receiveth wages, and gathereth fruit unto life eternal." At another time by martyrdom and confession in Christ's Name, for He says, "And he that hateth his life in this world shall keep it unto life eternal." And again, by preferring Christ to riches or kindred; "And every one that hath forsaken brethren, or sisters," &c., "shall inherit eternal life." Moreover it is by keeping the commandments, "Thou shalt not commit adultery: thou shalt not kill;" and the rest which follows; as He answered to him that came to Him, and said, "Good Master, what shall I do that I may have eternal life?" Further, it is by departing from evil works, and henceforth serving God; for Paul says, "But now being made free from sin, and become servants to God, ye have your fruit unto holiness, and the end everlasting life."

Catechetical Lectures, xviii.

Second Monday in Lent.

FAITHFUL STEWARDSHIP.
S. Chrysostom.

"It is required in stewards that a man be found faithful;" that is, that he do not appropriate to himself his master's goods, that he do not as a master lay claim for himself, but administer as a steward. For a steward's part is to administer well the things committed to his charge; not to say that his master's things are his own; but on the contrary, that his own are his master's. Let every one think on these things, both he that hath power in speech, and he that possesses wealth; namely, that he hath been intrusted with a master's goods, and that they are not his own; let him not keep them with himself, nor set them down to his own account, but let him impute them unto God Who gave them all. Wouldest thou see faithful stewards? Hear what saith Peter, "Why look ye so earnestly on us, as though by our own power or holiness we had made this man to walk?" Unto Cornelius also he saith, "We also are men of like passions with you;" and unto Christ Himself, "Lo! we have left all and followed Thee." And Paul no less, when he had said, "I laboured more abundantly than they all," added, "Yet not I, but the grace of God which was with me." Elsewhere also, setting himself strongly against the same persons, he said, "For what hast thou which thou didst not receive?" For thou hast nothing of thine own, neither wealth, nor speech, nor life itself; for this also is surely the Lord's. Wherefore when necessity calls, do thou lay down this also. But if thou doatest on life, and being ordered to lay it down refusest, thou art no longer a faithful steward. "And how is it possible, when God calls, to resist?" Well, that is just what I say too: and on this very account do I chiefly admire the Loving-kindness of God, that the things which He is able, even against thy will to take from thee, these He willeth not to be paid in by thee unwillingly, that thou mayest have a reward besides. For instance, He can take away life without thy consent, that thou mayest say with Paul, "I die daily." He can take away thy glory without thy consent, and bring thee low: but He will have it from thee with thine own good will, that thou mayest have a recompence. He can make thee poor, though unwilling, but He will have thee willingly become such, that He may weave crowns for thee. Seest thou God's mercy to man? Seest thou our own brutish stupidity?

What if thou art come to great dignity? Be not high-minded. Thou hast not acquired the glory, but God hath put it on thee. As if it were another's, therefore, use it sparingly; neither abusing it, nor using it upon unsuitable things, nor puffed up, nor appropriating it unto thyself; but esteem thyself to be poor and inglorious. For never, hadst thou been intrusted with a king's purple to keep, never would it have become thee to abuse the robe and spoil it, but with the more exactness to keep it for the giver. Is utterance given thee? Be not puffed up; be not arrogant; for the gracious gift is not thine. Be not grudging about thy Master's goods, but distribute them among thy fellow servants; and neither be thou elated with these things as if they were thine own, nor be sparing as to the distribution of them. Again, if thou hast children, they are God's which thou hast. If such be thy thought, thou wilt both be thankful for having them, and if bereft thou wilt not take it hard. Such was Job when he said, "The Lord gave, the Lord hath taken away."

For we have all things from Christ. Both existence itself we have through Him, and life, and breath, and light, and air, and earth. And if He were to exclude us from any one of these, we are lost and undone. For "we are strangers and sojourners." And all this about *mine* and *thine* is bare words only, and doth not stand for things. For if thou do but say, the house is thine, it is a word without a reality: since the very air, earth, matter, are the Creator's; and so art thou too thyself, who hath framed it; and all other things also. But supposing the use to be thine, even this is uncertain, not on account of death alone, but also before death, because of the instability of things.

These things then continually picturing to ourselves, let us live strict lives, and we shall gain two of the greatest advantages. For first, we shall be thankful both when we have, and when we are bereaved, and we shall not be enslaved to things which are fleeting by, and things not our own. For whether it be wealth that He taketh, He hath taken but His Own; or honour, or glory, or the body, or life itself: be it that He taketh away thy son, it is not thy son that He hath taken, but His Own servant. For thou formedst him not, but He made him. Thou didst but minister to his appearing, the whole was God's own work. Let us give thanks therefore that we have been counted worthy to be His ministers in this matter. But what? Wouldest thou have had him for ever? This again proves thee grudging, and ignorant that it was another's child which thou hadst, and not thine own. As therefore those who part resignedly are but aware that they have what was not theirs; so whoever gives way to grief, is in fact counting the king's property his own. For if we are not our own, how can they be ours? I say, *we*: for in two ways we are His, both on account of our creation, and also on account of the faith. Wherefore David saith, "My substance is with Thee;" and Paul too, "For in Him we live and move and have our being;" and plying the argument about the faith, he says, "Ye are not your own, and ye are bought with a price." For all things are God's. When then He calls, and chooses to take, let us not, like grudging servants, fly from the reckoning, nor purloin our Master's goods. Thy soul is not thine, and how can thy wealth be thine? How is it then that thou spendest on what is unnecessary the things that are not thine? Knowest thou not that for this we are soon to be put on our trial, that is, if we have used them badly? But seeing that they are not ours but our Master's, it were right to expend them upon our fellow-servants. It is worth considering that the omission of this was the charge brought against the rich man, and against those also who had not given food to the Lord.

Say not then, "I am but spending mine own, and of mine own I live delicately." It is not of thine own, but of other men's. Other men's, I say, because such is thine own choice; for God's Will is that these things should be thine, which have been intrusted unto thee on behalf of thy brethren. Now the things which are not thine own become thine, if thou spend them upon others: but if thou spend on thyself unsparingly, thine own things become no longer thine. For since thou usest them cruelly, and sayest, "That my own things should be altogether spent on my own enjoyment, is fair;" therefore I call them not thine own. For they are common to thee and thy fellow-servants; just as the sun is common, the air, the earth, and all the rest. For as in the case of the body, each ministration belongs both to the whole body and to each several member; but when it is applied to one single member only, it destroys the proper function of that very member: so also it comes to pass in the case of wealth. And that what I say may be made plainer, the food of the body which is given in common to the members, should it pass into one member, even to that it turns out alien in the end. For when it cannot be digested, nor afford nourishment, even to that part I say, it becomes alien. But if it be made common, both that part and all the rest have it as their own.

So also in regard to wealth. If you enjoy it alone, you too have lost it; for you will not reap its reward. But if you possess it jointly with the rest, then will it be more your own, and then will you reap the benefit of it. Seest thou not that the hands minister, and the mouth softens, and the stomach receives? Doth the stomach say, Since I have received, I ought to keep it all? Then do not thou, I pray, in regard to riches, use this language; for it belongs to the receiver to impart. As then it is a vice in the stomach to retain the food and not to distribute it, (for it is injurious to the whole body,) so it is a vice in those that are rich to keep to themselves what they have. For this destroys both themselves and others. Again, the eye receives all the light; but it doth not itself alone retain it, but enlightens the entire body. For it is not its nature to keep it to itself, so long as it is an eye. Again the nostrils are sensible of perfume, but they do not keep it all to themselves, but transmit it to the brain, and affect the stomach with a sweet savour, and by these means refresh the entire man. The feet alone walk; but they move not away themselves only, but transfer also the whole body. In like manner do thou. Whatsoever thou hast been intrusted withal, keep it not to thyself alone, since thou art doing harm to the whole, and to thyself more than all.

And not in the case of the limbs only may one see

this occurring; for the smith also, if he chose to impart of his craft to no one, ruins both himself and all other crafts. Likewise the cordwainer, the husbandman, the baker, and every one of those who pursue any necessary calling; if he chose not to communicate to any one the results of his art, will ruin not the others only, but himself also with them.

And why do I say the rich? For the poor too, if they followed after the wickedness of you who are covetous and rich, would injure you very greatly, and soon make you poor; yea rather they would quite destroy you, were they in great want unwilling to impart of their own; the tiller of the ground (for instance) of the labour of his hands, the sailor of the gain from his voyages; the soldier of his distinction won in the wars.

Wherefore if nothing else can, let this at least put you to shame, and do you imitate their benevolence. Dost thou impart none of thy wealth unto any? Then shouldest thou not receive any thing from another; in which case the world will be turned upside down. For in every thing to give and receive is the principle of numerous blessings: in seeds, in scholars, in arts. For if any one desire to keep his art to himself, he subverts both himself and the whole course of things. And the husbandman, if he bury and keep the seeds in his house, will bring about a grievous famine. So also the rich man, if he act thus in regard of his wealth, will destroy himself before the poor, heaping up the fire of hell more grievous upon his own head.

Therefore as teachers, however many scholars

they have, impart some of their lore unto each; so let thy possession be, many to whom thou hast done good. And let all say, " Such an one he freed from poverty, such an one from dangers. Such an one would have perished, had he not, next to the grace of God, enjoyed thy patronage. This man's disease thou didst cure, another thou didst rid of false accusation, another being a stranger ye took in, another being naked ye clothed." Wealth inexhaustible and many treasures are not so good as such sayings. They draw all men's gaze more powerfully than your golden vestments, and horses and slaves. For these make a man appear even odious, they cause him to be hated as a common foe; but the former proclaim him as a common father and benefactor. And what is greatest of all, favour from God waits on thee in every part of thy proceedings. What I mean is, let one man say, he helped to portion out my daughter; another, and he afforded my son the means of taking his station among men; another, he made my calamity to cease; another, he delivered me from dangers. Better than golden crowns are words such as these, that a man should have in his city innumerable persons to proclaim his beneficence. Voices such as these are pleasanter far and sweeter than the voices of the heralds marching before the archers; to be called saviour, benefactor, defender, (the very names of God,) and not covetous, proud, insatiate and mean. Let us not, I beseech you, let us not have a fancy for any of these latter titles, but the contrary. For if these spoken on earth, make one so splendid and illustrious; when they are written in heaven, and God proclaims them on the day that shall come, think what renown, what splendour thou shalt enjoy! Which may it be the lot of us all to obtain, through the Grace and Loving-kindness of our Lord Jesus Christ, &c.

In 1 Cor. Hom. x.

Second Tuesday in Lent.

ON EXAMPLE. S. Chrysostom.

LET this be our way of overpowering our adversaries, and of conducting our warfare against them: and let us before all words, astound them by our way of life. For this is the main battle, this is the unanswerable argument, the argument from actions. For though we give ten thousand precepts of philosophy in words, if we do not exhibit a life better than theirs, the gain is nothing. For it is not what is said that draws their attention, but their enquiry is, what we *do;* and they say, "Do thou first obey thine own words, and then admonish others. But if while thou sayest, 'Infinite are the blessings in the world to come,' thou seem thyself nailed down to this world, just as if none such existed, thy works to me are more credible than thy words. For when I see thee seizing other men's goods, weeping immoderately over the departed, doing ill in many other things, how shall I believe thee that there is a resurrection?" And what if men utter not this in words? They think it, and turn it often in their minds. And this is what stays the unbelievers from becoming Christians.

Let us win them therefore by our life. Many, even among the untaught, have in that way astounded the minds of philosophers, as having exhibited in themselves also that philosophy which lies in deeds, and uttered a voice clearer than a trumpet by their mode of life and self-denial. For this is stronger than the tongue.. But when I say, "one ought not to bear malice," and then do all manner of evils to mine adversary, how shall I be able by words to win him, while by my deeds I am frightening him away? Let us catch them then by our mode of life; and by their souls let us build up the Church, and of these let us amass our wealth. There is nothing to weigh against a soul, not even the whole world. So that although thou give countless treasure unto the poor, thou wilt do no such work as he who converteth one soul. "For he that taketh forth the precious from the vile shall be as My mouth:" so He speaks. (Jer. xv. 19.) A great good it is, I grant, to have mercy on the poor; but it is nothing equal to withdrawing them from error. For he that doth this resembles Paul and Peter; we being permitted to take up their Gospel, not with perils such as theirs, with endurance of famines and pestilences, and all other evils, (for the present is a season of peace,) but so as to display that diligence which cometh of zeal. For even while we sit at home we may practise this kind of feeling. Whoso hath a friend or relation or inmate of his house, these things let him say, these do: and he shall be like Peter and Paul. And why do I say Peter and Paul? He shall be the Mouth of Christ. For He saith, "He that taketh forth the precious from the vile shall be as My Mouth." And though thou persuade not to-day, to-morrow thou shalt persuade. And though thou never persuade, thou shalt have thine own reward in full. And though thou persuade not all, a few out of many thou mayest; since neither did the apostles persuade all men that are; but still they discoursed with all, and for all they have their reward. For not according to the result of the things that are well done, but according to the intention of the doers, is God wont to assign the crowns: though thou pay down but two farthings, He receiveth them; and what He did in the case of the widow, the same will He do also in the case of those who teach. Do not thou then, because thou canst not save the world, despise the few; nor though longing after the greater things, withdraw thyself from the lesser. If thou canst not a hundred, take thou charge of ten; if thou canst not ten, despise not even five; if thou canst not five, do not overlook one; and if thou canst not one, neither so despair, nor keep back what may be done by thee. Seest thou not how in matters of trade, they who are so employed make their profit not only with gold but with silver also? For if we are not come to slighting the little things, we shall keep hold also of the great. But if we despise the small, neither shall we easily lay hand upon the other. Thus individuals become rich, gathering both small and great; and so let us act, that in all things enriched, we may obtain the kingdom of heaven; through the Grace and Lovingkindness of our Lord Jesus Christ, with Whom unto the Father, together with the Holy Spirit, be glory, power, honour, now, henceforth and for evermore. Amen.

In Cor. Hom. iii.

Third Wednesday in Lent.

FASTING.   S. CHRYSOSTOM.

S. PAUL says, "Put on the whole armour of God." Hast thou observed the wrestler? Hast thou observed the soldier? If thou art a wrestler, it is necessary for thee to engage in the conflict naked. If a soldier, it behoves thee to stand armed at all points for the battle. How then are both these things possible, to be naked, and yet not naked; to be clothed, and yet not clothed? How? I will tell thee. Divest thyself of worldly cares, and thou hast become a wrestler. Put on the spiritual armour, and thou hast become a soldier. Strip thyself of worldly thoughts, for the season is one of wrestling. Clothe thyself with a spiritual panoply, for we have a heavy warfare to wage with demons. Therefore also it is needful we should be naked, so as to offer nothing that the devil may take hold of, while he is wrestling with us; and to be fully armed at all points, so as on no side to receive a deadly blow. Cultivate thy soul. Cut away the thorns, sow the word of godliness. Nurse with much care the fair plants of divine wisdom, and thou hast become a husbandman. Sharpen thy sickle, which thou hast blunted through gluttony; sharpen it by fasting. Attempt the pathway which leads towards Heaven, rugged and narrow as it is, attempt it, and proceed onwards. And how mayest thou be able to do these things? By mortifying thy body, and bringing it into subjection. Keep down the waves of inordinate desires; repel the tempest of evil thoughts; preserve the bark; display much skill, and thou hast become a pilot. And the fast is our groundwork and guide to all this.

I speak not indeed of such a fast as many keep, but of real fasting; not merely an abstinence from meats, but from sins too. For the nature of a fast is such, that it does not suffice to deliver those who practise it, unless it be done according to a suitable law. "For the wrestler," it is said, "is not crowned unless he strive lawfully." (2 Tim. ii. 15.)

To the end then, that when we have gone through

the labour of fasting, we forfeit not the crown of fasting, we should understand how, and after what manner, it is necessary to conduct this business; since that Pharisee also fasted, but afterwards went down empty, and destitute of the fruit of fasting. (S. Luke xviii.) The publican fasted not, and yet he was accepted in preference to him who had fasted; in order that thou mayest learn that fasting is unprofitable, except all other duties follow with it. The Ninevites fasted, and won the favour of God. (Jonah iii. 10.) The Jews fasted too, and profited nothing, nay, they departed with blame. (Isa. lviii. 3, 7.) Since then the danger in fasting is so great to those who do not know how they ought to fast, we should learn the laws of this exercise, in order that we may not "run uncertainly," nor "beat the air," nor while we are fighting contend with a shadow. Fasting is a medicine, but a medicine though it be never so profitable, becomes frequently useless by the unskilfulness of him who employs it. And if when the body needs healing, such exactness is required on our part, much more ought we, when our care is about the soul, and we seek to heal the distempers of the mind, to look, and to search into every particular with the utmost accuracy.

Fasting consists not in abstinence from food, (only,) but in a separation from sinful practices; since he who limits his fasting only to an abstinence from meats, is one who especially disparages it. Dost thou fast? Give me proof of it by thy works. Is it said by what works? If thou seest a poor man, take pity on' him. If thou seest an enemy, be reconciled to him; if thou seest a friend gaining honour, envy him not. Let not the mouth only fast, but also the eye, and the ear, and the feet and the hands, and all the members of our bodies. Let the hands fast, by being pure from rapine and avarice. Let the feet fast, by ceasing from running to forbidden pleasures. Let the eyes fast, being taught never to fix themselves on curious or unholy delights. Let the ear fast also, the fasting of the ear is not to receive evil speakings and calumnies.

Let the mouth too fast from disgraceful speeches and railing. For what doth it profit if we abstain from birds and fishes, and yet bite and devour our brethren? Thou hast not fixed thy teeth in the flesh, but thou hast fixed the slander in the soul; thou hast harmed in a thousand ways, thyself, and thy neighbour, and many others, for in slandering a neighbour thou hast made him who listens to the slander worse; for should he be a wicked man, he becomes more careless when he finds a partner in his wickedness; and should he be a just man, he is lifted up to arrogance, and puffed up; being led on by the sin of others to imagine great things concerning himself.

It is not therefore to go through the fast if we merely go through the time, but if we go through it with amendment of manners. Let us consider this; whether we have become more diligent, whether we have corrected any of our defects; whether we have washed away our sins? It is common for every one to ask in Lent, how many weeks each has fasted; and some may be heard saying that they have fasted two, others three, and others that they have fasted the whole of the weeks. But what advantage is it, if we have gone through the fast devoid of good works? If another says, "I have fasted the whole of Lent," do thou say, "I had an enemy, but I was reconciled; I had a custom of evil-speaking, but I put a stop to it; I had a custom of swearing, but I have broken through this evil practice." It is of no advantage to merchants, if they have gone over a great extent of ocean, but if they have sailed with a freight and much merchandise. The fast will profit us nothing, if we pass through it as a mere matter of course, without any result. If we practise a mere abstinence from meats, when the forty days are past the fast is over too. But if we abstain from sins, this still remains, even when the fast has gone by, and will be from this time a continual advantage to us, and will here render us no small recompence, before we attain unto the kingdom of heaven. For as he who is living in iniquity, even before hell hath punishment, being stung by his conscience; so the man who is rich in good works even before the kingdom, attains exceeding joy, in that he is nourished with blessed hopes.

S. Chrysos. De Stat. Homil. iii. 7—12, and xvi. 16.

Third Thursday in Lent.

CHRIST'S SPIRITUAL CURES.
S. Augustine.

Christ now worketh greater cures, on account of which He disdained not formerly to exhibit lesser ones. For as the soul is better than the body, so is the saving health of the soul, better than the health of the body. The blind body doth not now open its eyes by a miracle of the Lord, but the blinded heart openeth its eyes to the Word of the Lord. The mortal corpse doth not now rise again, but the soul doth rise again which lay dead in a living body. The deaf ears of the body are not now opened; but how many have the ears of their heart closed, which yet fly open at the penetrating Word of God, so that they believe, who did not believe, and they live well, who did live evilly, and they obey, who did not obey; and we say, "Such a man is become a believer," and we wonder to hear of them whom once we had known as hardened. Why then dost thou marvel at one who now believes, who is living innocently, and serving God, but because thou dost behold him seeing whom thou hadst known to be blind; dost behold him living whom thou hadst known to be dead; dost behold him hearing whom thou hadst known to be deaf? For consider that there are who are dead in another than the ordinary sense, of whom the Lord spake to a certain man who delayed to follow the Lord, because he wished to bury his father. "Let the dead," said He, "bury their dead." Surely these dead buriers are not dead in body; for if this were so, they could not bury dead bodies. Yet doth He call them dead; where, but in the soul within? For as we may often see in a household, itself sound and well, the master of the same house lying dead, so in a sound body do many carry a dead soul within; and these the Apostle arouses thus, "Awake, thou that sleepest, and arise from the dead, and Christ shall give thee light." (Eph. v. 14.) It is the same Who giveth light to the blind, that awakeneth the dead. For it is with His Voice that the cry is made by the Apostle to the dead, "Awake, thou that sleepest." And the blind will be enlightened with light, when he shall have risen again. And how many deaf men did the Lord see before His Eyes, when He said, "He that hath ears to hear, let him hear." For who was standing before Him without his bodily ears? What other ears then did He seek for, but those of the inner man?

Again what eyes did He look for when He spake to those who saw indeed, but who saw only with the eyes of the flesh? For when Philip said to Him, "Lord, shew us the Father, and it sufficeth us," he understood indeed that if the Father were shewn him, it might well suffice him; but how would the Father suffice him when He that was equal to the Father sufficed not? And why did He not suffice? Because He was not seen? And why was He not seen? Because the eye whereby He might be seen was not yet made whole. For this namely, that the Lord was seen in the flesh with the outward eyes, not only the disciples who honoured Him saw, but also the Jews who crucified Him. He then Who wished to be seen in another way, sought for other eyes. And therefore it was that to him who said, "Shew us the Father, and it sufficeth us," He answered, "Have I been so long time with you, and yet hast thou not known Me, Philip? He who hath seen Me hath seen the Father also." And that He might in the meanwhile heal the eyes of faith, he has first of all instructions given him regarding faith, that so he might attain to sight. And lest Philip should think that he was to conceive of God under the same form in which he then saw the Lord Jesus Christ in the body, He immediately subjoined; "Believest thou not that I am in the Father, and the Father in Me?" He had already said, "He who hath seen Me hath seen the Father also." But Philip's eye was not yet sound enough to see the Father, nor consequently to see the Son, Who is Himself Coequal with the Father. And so Jesus Christ took in hand to cure, and with the medicines and salve of faith to strengthen, the eyes of his mind, which as yet were weak and unable to behold so great a light, and He said, "Believest thou not that I am in the Father, and the Father in Me?" Let not him then, who cannot yet see what the Lord will one day shew him, seek first to see what he is to believe; but let him first believe that the eye by which he is to see may be healed. For it was only the form of the servant which was exhibited to the eyes of servants; because if He "Who thought it not robbery to be equal with God," could have been now seen as equal with God by those whom He wished to be healed, He would not have needed to " empty Himself, and to take the form of a servant." But because there was no way whereby God could be seen, but whereby man could be seen there was; therefore He Who was God was made Man, that that which was seen might heal that whereby He was not seen. For He saith Himself in another place, "Blessed are the pure in heart, for they shall see God." Philip might of course have answered and said, "Lord, lo I see Thee; is the Father such as I see Thee to be? forasmuch as Thou hast said, He who hath seen Me hath seen the Father also?" But before Philip answered thus, or perhaps before he so much as thought it, when the Lord had said, "He who hath seen Me hath seen the Father also," He immediately added, "Believest thou not that I am in the Father, and the Father in Me?" For with that eye he could not yet see either the Father, or the Son that is equal with the Father; but that his eye might be healed for seeing, he was to be anointed unto believing. So then before thou seest what thou canst not now see, believe what as yet thou seest not. "Walk by faith," that thou mayest attain to sight. Sight will not gladden him in his home whom faith consoleth not by the way. For so says the Apostle,

"As long as we are in the body, we are in pilgrimage from the Lord." (2 Cor. v. 6.) And he subjoins immediately why we are still in pilgrimage, though we have now believed; "For we walk by faith," he says, "not by sight."

Our whole business then, brethren, in this life, is to heal this eye of the heart whereby God may be seen. To this end are celebrated the Holy Mysteries; to this end is preached the Word of God; to this end are the moral exhortations of the Church, those, that is, that relate to the correction of manners, to the amendment of carnal lusts, to the renouncing the world, not in word only, but in a change of life; to this end is directed the whole aim of the Divine and Holy Scriptures, that the inner man may be purged of that which hinders us from the sight of God. For as the eye which is formed to see this temporal light, a light though heavenly, yet corporal, and manifest not to men only, but even to the meanest animals, (for for this the eye is formed, to see this light,) if any thing be thrown or fall into it, whereby it is disordered, is shut out from this light; and though it encompass the eye with its presence, yet the eye turns itself away from and is absent from it; and through its disordered condition is not only rendered absent from the light which is present, but the light, to see which it was formed, is even painful to it. So the eye of the heart too, when it is disordered and wounded, turns away from the light of righteousness, and dares not and cannot contemplate it.

And what is it that disorders the eye of the heart?

Evil desire, covetousness, injustice, worldly concupiscence, these disorder, blind, and close the eye of the heart. And yet when the eye of the body is out of order, how is the physician sought out, what an absence of all delay to open and cleanse it, that that may be healed whereby this outward light is seen! There is running to and fro, no one is still, no one loiters, if even the smallest straw fall into the eye. And God, it must be allowed, made the sun which we desire to see with sound eyes. Much brighter assuredly is He Who made it; nor is the light with which the eye of the mind is concerned of this kind at all. That light is eternal wisdom. God made thee, O man, after His Own Image. Would He give thee wherewithal to see the sun which He made, and not give thee wherewithal to see Him who made thee, when He made thee after His Own Image? He hath given thee this also; both hath He given thee. But much dost thou love these outward eyes, and despisest much that interior eye; it thou dost carry about bruised and wounded. Yea, it would be a punishment to thee, if thy Maker should wish to manifest Himself to thee; it would be a punishment to thine eye, before that it is cured and healed. For so Adam in Paradise sinned, and hid himself from the Face of God. As long then as he had the sound heart of a pure conscience, he rejoiced at the presence of God; when that eye was wounded by sin he began to dread the Divine light, he fled back into the darkness, and the thick covert of the trees, flying from the truth, and anxious for the shade.

Therefore, my brethren, since we too are born of him, and as the Apostle says, "In Adam all die," for we were all at first two persons ; if we were loth to obey the physician, that we might not be sick, let us obey Him now, that we may be delivered from sickness. The Physician gave us precepts when we were whole ; He gave us precepts that we might not need a physician. "They that are whole," He saith, "need not a physician, but they that are sick." When whole we despised these precepts, and by experience have felt how to our own destruction we despised His precepts. Now we are sick, we are in distress, we are on the bed of weakness, yet let us not despair. For because we could not come to the Physician, He hath vouchsafed to come Himself to us. Though despised by man when he was whole, He did not despise him when he was stricken. He did not leave off to give other precepts to the weak, who would not keep the first precepts, that he might not be weak ; as though He would say, "Assuredly thou hast by experience felt that I spake the truth when I said, Touch not this. Be healed then now at length, and recover the life thou hast lost. Lo, I am bearing thine infirmity : drink thou the bitter cup. For thou hast of thine own self made those My so sweet precepts which were given to thee when whole, so toilsome. They were despised, and so thy distress began ; cured thou canst not be, except thou drink the bitter cup, the cup of temptations, wherein this life abounds, the cup of tribulation, anguish, and sufferings. "Drink then," He says, "drink that thou mayest live." And that the sick man may not make answer, "I cannot; I cannot bear it, I will not drink," the Physician, all whole though He be, drinketh first, that the sick man may not hesitate to drink. For what bitterness is there in this cup, that He hath not drunk? If it be contumely, He heard it first when He drove out the devils, "He hath a devil, and by Beelzebub He casteth out devils." Whereupon in order to comfort the sick, He saith, "If they have called the Master of the house Beelzebub, how much more shall they call them of His household?"

If pains are this bitter cup, He was bound, scourged, and crucified. If death be this bitter cup, He died also. If infirmity shrink with horror from any particular kind of death, none was at that time more ignominious than the death of the cross. For it was not in vain that the Apostle, when setting forth His obedience, added, "made obedient unto death, even the death of the cross." (Phil. ii. 8.) Our Lord in doing these divine, and suffering these human things, instructs us by His bodily miracles, and bodily patience, that we may believe, and be made whole to behold those things invisible which the eye of the body hath no knowledge of.

The two blind men who sat by the wayside, cried out, "Have mercy on us, Thou Son of David." Now what is it, brethren, to "cry out" unto Christ, but to correspond to the grace of Christ by good works? This I say, brethren, lest haply we cry aloud with our voices, and in our lives be dumb. Who is he that crieth out to Christ that his inward blindness may be driven away by Christ as He is "passing by," that is, as He is dispensing to us those temporal sacraments, whereby we are instructed to receive the things which are eternal? Who is he that crieth out unto Christ? Whoso despiseth the world, crieth out unto Christ. Whoso saith, not with his tongue, but with his life, "The world is crucified unto me, and I unto the world," crieth out unto Christ. Whoso "disperseth abroad and giveth to the poor, that his righteousness may endure for ever," crieth out unto Christ. For let him that hears, and is not deaf to the sound, "Sell that ye have, and give to the poor; provide yourselves bags which wax not old, a treasure in the heavens that faileth not," let him as he hears the sound as it were of Christ's footsteps "passing by," cry out in response to this in his blindness, that is, let him do these things. Let his voice be in his actions. Let him begin to despise the world, to distribute to the poor his goods, to esteem as nothing worth what other men love; let him disregard injuries, not seek to be avenged; let him give his cheek to the smiters, let him pray for his enemies; if any one have taken away his goods, let him not ask for them again; if he have taken any thing from any man, let him restore fourfold.

When he shall begin to do all this, all his kinsmen, relations, and friends, will be in commotion. They who love this world will oppose him. "What madness this! you are too extreme! What! are not other men Christians? This is folly, this is madness!"

And other such like things do the multitude cry out to prevent the blind from crying out. The multitude rebuked them as they cried out, but did not overcome their cries. Let them who wish to be healed understand what they have to do. Jesus is also now "passing by;" let them who are by the wayside cry out. These are they "who know God with their lips, but their heart is far from Him;" these are they by the wayside, to whom as blinded in heart, Jesus gives His precepts. For when those passing things which Jesus did are recounted, Jesus is always represented to us as "passing by." For even unto the end of the world there will not be wanting "blind men sitting by the wayside." Need then there is that they who sit by the wayside should cry out. The multitude that was with the Lord would repress the crying out of those who were seeking for recovery. Brethren, do ye see my meaning? Evil and lukewarm Christians hinder good Christians who are truly earnest, and wish to do the commandments of God which are written in the Gospel. This multitude which is with the Lord hinders those who are crying out, hinders those, that is, who are doing well, that they may not by perseverance be healed. But let them cry out, and not faint; let them not be led away as if by the authority of numbers; let them not imitate those who live evil lives themselves, and are jealous of the good deeds of others. Let them not say, "Let us live as these so many live." Why not rather as the Gospel ordains? Why dost thou wish to live according to the remonstrances of the multitude who would hinder thee, and not after the steps of the Lord, "Who passeth by"? They will mock, and abuse, and call thee back; do thou cry out till thou reach the Ears of Jesus. For they who persevere in doing such things as Christ hath enjoined, and regard not the multitudes that hinder them, nor think much of their appearing to follow Christ, that is, of their being called Christians; but who love the light which Christ is about to restore to them, more than they fear the uproar of those who are hindering them; they shall on no account be separated from Him, and Jesus will "stand still," and make them whole.

See what crowds there are which "rebuke the blind as they cry out!" But let them not deter you, whosoever among this crowd desire to be healed; for there are many Christians in name, and in works ungodly; let them not deter you from good works. Cry out amid the crowds that are restraining you and calling you back, and insulting you, whose lives are evil. Cry out amidst the very crowds, despair not of reaching the ears of the Lord. For the blind men in the Gospel did not cry out in that quarter where no crowd was, so that they might be heard in that direction, where there was no impediment from persons hindering them. Amidst the very crowds they cried out, and yet the Lord heard them. And so also do ye now amidst sinners and sensual men, amidst the lovers of the vanities of the world, there cry out that the Lord may heal you. Consider, brethren, how in the crowd which was hindering them from crying out, even there were they who cried out made whole. For observe this too, holy brethren, what it is to persevere in crying out. I will speak of what many as well as myself have experienced in Christ's Name, for the Church does not cease to give birth to such as these. When any Christian has begun to live well, to be fervent in good works, and to despise the world; in this newness of his life he is exposed to the animadversions and contradictions of cold Christians. But if he persevere, and get the better of them by his endurance, and faint not in good works, those very same persons who before hindered him will now respect him.

Homil. on the New Testament, xxxviii.

Third Friday in Lent.

REPENTANCE BEFORE COMMUNION.
S. PACIAN.

BRETHREN, I call on you, who having committed crimes, refuse penance: you I say, timid after being shameless, modest after sinning: who blush not to sin, yet blush to confess; who with evil conscience touch the holy things of God, and fear not the altar of the Lord; who come to the hands of the priest, who come in the sight of angels with the confidence of innocence; who insult the Divine patience; who bring to God (as if, because silent, He knew not) a polluted soul and a profane body. Hear first what the Lord hath done, and then what He hath said. When the people of the Hebrews were bringing back the ark of the Lord to Jerusalem, Uzzah from the house of Amminadab the Israelite, who had touched the side of the ark without having examined his conscience, was slain; and yet he had drawn near, not to take any thing from it, but to hold it when leaning through the stumbling of the kine. So great a care was there of reverence towards God, that He endured not bold hands even in help. The same also the Lord crieth, saying, "And as for the flesh, all that be clean shall eat thereof. But the soul that eateth of the flesh of the sacrifice of peace-offerings, having uncleanness upon him, that soul shall be cut off from his people." (Lev. vii. 19.) Are these things old, and happen they not now? What then? Hath God ceased to care for what concerns us? Hath He withdrawn out of view of the world, and doth He look down upon no one from heaven? Is His long-suffering ignorance? God forbid, thou wilt say, He seeth then what we do, but He waiteth indeed and endureth, and granteth a season for repentance, and alloweth His Christ to put off the end, lest they quickly perish whom He hath redeemed. Understand well, thou sinner, thou art beheld by God. Thou canst appease Him if thou wilt. But grant that it is a thing of old that the unclean were not permitted to approach the table of God: open the writings of the Apostles, and learn what is of later date.

In the first Epistle to the Corinthians S. Paul hath inserted these words. "Whosoever," he saith, "shall eat this Bread, and drink this Cup of the Lord, unworthily, shall be guilty of the Body and Blood of the Lord." So likewise below: "For he that eateth and drinketh unworthily, eateth and drinketh damnation to himself, not discerning the Lord's Body. For this cause many are weak and sickly among you, and many sleep. For if we would judge ourselves, we should not be judged. But when we are judged we are chastened of the Lord, that we should not be condemned with the world." Do ye tremble or not? "Shall be guilty," he saith, "of the Body and Blood of the Lord?" One guilty as to human life could not be absolved; doth he escape who violates the Body of the Lord? "He that eateth and drinketh unworthily," he saith, "eateth and drinketh damnation to himself." Awake, O sinner; fear judgment within thee if thou hast done any such thing. "For this cause," saith he, "many are weak and sickly among you, and many sleep." If then any one fears not the future, let him now at least dread present sickness and present death. "But when we are judged," he saith, "we are chastened of the Lord, that we should not be condemned with the world." Rejoice, O sinner, if in this life thou art either cut off by death, or wasted by sickness, that thou be not punished in the life to come. See how great wickedness he committeth who cometh when unworthy to the altar, to whom it is reckoned a remedy, if he either labours under sickness, or is destroyed by death!

I beseech you, brethren, by that Lord from Whom no secrets are hid, cease from hiding the wounds of your consciences. The wise, when sick, fear not the physician, and shall the sinner fear? Shall the sinner blush to purchase everlasting life by present shame, and withdraw his ill-concealed wounds from the Lord when He stretcheth forth His Hands? And hath he any thing whereat to blush before the priest, who hath injured the Lord? By not giving way to shame thou wouldest gain more through its loss. But if ye are ashamed that the eyes of your brethren should see, fear not those who are partners in your misfortune. No body is glad at the sufferings of its own members; it grieves with them, and labours with them for a remedy. In one and two is the Church, and in the Church is Christ. And he therefore who hides not his sins from the brethren, assisted by the tears of the Church, is absolved by Christ.

And now I would address those who, well and wisely confessing their sins, [under the name of penance] neither know what repentance is, nor what the cure for their wounds, and are like those who lay bare indeed their wounds and swellings, and acknowledge them also to the physician who sitteth by; but when warned what is to be applied, neglect it, and refuse what they have to take. This is just as if one should say, "Lo! I am sick; Lo! I am wounded, but I wish not to be cured." Such it is, but see a thing still more foolish.

Another disease is added to the original cause, and a new wound inflicted, all that is just contrary is applied, all that is hurtful is drunken. What then shall the priest do who is compelled to cure? It is late in such cases. If however there is any one of you who can bear to be cut and cauterized, it can still be done. Behold the knife of the Prophet; "Turn unto the Lord your God," he saith, "with all your heart, and with fasting, and with weeping, and with mourning: and rend your heart." Fear not this cutting, most beloved. David bore it. He lay in filthy ashes, and was disfigured by a covering of rough sackcloth. He who had once been accustomed to gems and purple, bid his soul in fasting; he whom seas, whom woods, whom streams served, and the land bringing forth the promised wealth, wasted in floods of tears those eyes with which he had beheld the glory of God; the ancestor of Mary, the ruler also of the Jewish kingdom, confessed himself unhappy and miserable.

The king of Babylon performs penitence, forsaken of all, and is worn away by seven years of squalidness. Yet this punishment commends him to God, and restores him to the kingdom once his own. Whom men shuddered at, God received, blessed through this very calamity of a severer discipline. Behold the cutting which I promised. Whoso shall be able to endure it shall be healed.

I will yet apply fire from the cautery of the Apostle. Let us see whether ye can bear it. "I have judged," he saith, "when ye are gathered together, and my spirit, with the power of our Lord Jesus Christ, to deliver such an one unto Satan for the destruction of the flesh, that the spirit may be saved in the day of the Lord Jesus." What say ye, penitents? Where is the destruction of your flesh? Is it that in the very time of penance ye walk abroad in greater pomp, full from the feast, with well studied attire? Men and women are not ashamed to be dwelling in marble, weighed down with gold, sweeping along in silk, glowing with scarlet.

I can bear it no longer, brethren. Daniel with his fellows, covered with sackcloth and ashes, pale through fasting, speaketh thus: "We have sinned, we have committed iniquity, we have done wickedly, we have transgressed Thy precepts and Thy judgments." Of Azariah also the Divine Scripture saith, "Azariah stood up and prayed, and opening his mouth, made confession to God with his fellows." David himself saith, "Every night wash I my bed, and water my couch with my tears." But we, what of such sort do we? what like to this? I speak not of those things which we gather together in heaps, by trafficking, merchandizing, ravening; by hunting out gains abroad, and lusts at home; by doing nothing simply, giving nothing to the poor, forgiving nothing to brethren. But not even the daily duties do we observe: to weep, namely, in sight of the Church, to mourn our lost life in humble garb, to fast, to pray, to fall prostrate; to refuse luxury, to say if one invite to a feast, "These things for the happy! I have sinned against the Lord, and am in danger of perishing eternally. What have I to do with feasting who have injured the Lord?" And besides this, to hold the poor man by the hand, to intreat the prayers of the widows, to fall down before the Priests, to ask the intreaties of the interceding Church, to essay all sooner than perish.

I know that some of your brethren and sisters wrap themselves in hair-cloth, lie in ashes, and study late fastings; not yet perhaps, have they so sinned. Why speak of brethren? The wild goats we are told know what will cure themselves. I have heard that when pierced with the poisoned arrow they traverse the Cretan forests, until plucking the stalk of the dittany, they with the poisonous liquid of the healing juice expel from their bodies the ejected darts. We repel "the fiery darts of the devil" with no juice of penance, with no plant of confession. The swallow knoweth how by her own swallow-wort to give sight to her blinded young. We cure the lost light of the mind by no root of severe discipline. Lo! man, neither like the goat nor the swallow, is jealous of his own blindness and malady!

Now brethren consider what we promised at the close, what reward, or contrariwise what end will follow these works. The Spirit of the Lord threateneth delicate sinners who do not penance, saying, "They received not the love of the truth, that they might be saved. And for this cause God shall send

H

them the working of delusion, that they should believe a lie: that they all might be damned who believed not the truth, but had pleasure in unrighteousness." Also the Apocalypse thus speaketh, "How much she hath glorified herself, and lived deliciously, so much torment and sorrow give her." And the Apostle Paul saith, "Not knowing that the goodness of God leadeth thee to repentance, but after thy hardness treasured up unto thyself wrath against the day of wrath, and revelation of the righteous judgment of God."

Fear then, most dearly beloved, these righteous judgments. Leave off error: condemn delicate living. The last time is now hastening on. Darkness and hell are opening their enlarged bosoms for the wicked.

Consider in the Gospel the rich man, as yet suffering under the tortures of the soul only. What then shall be those exceeding tortures of the restored bodies! What gnashing of teeth therein! What weeping! Remember brethren, "there is no confession in the grave," nor can penance there be assigned, when the season for penitence is exhausted. Hasten whilst ye are alive, "whilst ye are on the way with your adversary." Lo, we fear the fires of this world, and we shrink back from the iron claws of tortures! Compare them with the hands of everlasting tortures, and the forked flames which never die!

By the faith of the Church, by mine own anxiety, by the souls of all in common, I adjure and intreat you brethren, not to be ashamed in this work, not to be slack to seize, as soon as ye may, the proffered remedies of salvation; to bring your souls down by mourning, to clothe the body with sackcloth, to sprinkle it with ashes, to macerate yourselves by fasting, to wean yourselves with sorrow, to gain the aid of the prayers of many. In proportion as ye have not been sparing in your own chatisement, will God spare you. For "He is merciful and long-suffering, of great pity, and repenteth Him against the evil He hath inflicted." Behold, I promise, I engage, if ye return to your Father with true satisfaction, erring no more, adding nothing to former sins, saying also some humble and mournful words, as, "Father, we have sinned before Thee, and are no more worthy to be called Thy sons;" straightway shall leave you both that filthy herd, and the unseemly food of husks. Straightway on your return shall the robe be put upon you, and the ring adorn you, and your Father's embrace again receive you. Lo, He saith Himself, "I have no pleasure in the death of the wicked; but that he turn from his way and live." And again He saith, "Shall they fall and not arise? Shall they turn away, and not return?" And the Apostle saith, "God is able to make him stand."

The Apocalypse also threateneth the seven Churches unless they should repent; nor would He indeed threaten the impenitent, unless He also pardoned the penitent. God Himself also saith, "Remember therefore from whence thou art fallen and repent."

And again, "When thou shalt return and mourn, then shalt thou be saved, and know where thou hast been." And let no one so despair of the vileness of a sinful soul, as to believe that God hath no longer need of him. The Lord willeth not that one of us should perish. Even those of little worth, and the least, are sought after. If ye believe not, see. Lo, in the Gospel the piece of silver is sought after, and when found is shewn unto the neighbours! The poor sheep, although to be carried back on his lowly stooping shoulders, is not burdensome to the shepherd. Over one sinner that repenteth the Angels in Heaven rejoice, and the celestial choir is glad. Come then, thou sinner: cease not to ask! Thou seest where there is joy over thy return! Amen.

Parænesis ad Pœn.

Third Saturday in Lent.

REGULATION OF VIRTUES. S. GREGORY.

(AN ALLEGORICAL INTERPRETATION OF PART OF THE FIRST CHAPTER OF JOB.)

"JOB'S seven sons went and feasted in their houses, every one his day."

The sons feast in their houses when the several virtues feed the mind after their proper sort; and it is well said, "Every one his day," for each son's day is the shining of each virtue. Briefly to unfold then these same gifts of sevenfold grace, wisdom has one day, understanding another day, counsel another, fortitude another, knowledge another, piety another, fear another, for it is not the same thing to be wise that it is to understand; for many indeed are wise in the things of eternity, but cannot in any sort understand them. Wisdom therefore gives a feast in its day in that it refreshes the mind with the hope and assurance of eternal things. Understanding spreads a feast in its day, forasmuch as in that it penetrates the truths heard, refreshing the heart, it lights up its darkness. Counsel gives a feast in its day, in that while it stays us from acting precipitately, it makes the mind to be full of reason. Fortitude gives a feast in its day, in that whereas it has no fear of adversity, it sets the viands of confidence before the alarmed soul. Knowledge prepares a feast in her day, in that in the mind's belly she overcomes the emptiness of ignorance. Piety sets forth a feast in its day, in that it satisfies the bowels of the heart with deeds of mercy. Fear makes a feast in its day, in that whereas it keeps down the mind, that it may not pride itself in the present things, it strengthens it with the meat of hope for the future

But I see that this point requires searching into in this feasting of the sons, namely, that by turns they feed one another. For each particular virtue is to the last degree destitute, unless one virtue lends its support to another. For wisdom is less worth if it lacks understanding, and understanding is wholly useless if it be not based upon wisdom, in that whilst it penetrates the higher mysteries without the counterpoise of wisdom, its own lightness is only lifting it up to meet with the heavier fall. Counsel is worthless when the strength of fortitude is lacking thereto, since what it finds out by turning the thing over, from want of strength it never carries on so far as to the perfecting in deed, and fortitude is very much broken down, if it be not supported by counsel, since the greater the power which it perceives itself to have, so much the more miserably does this virtue rush headlong into ruin, without the governance of reason. Knowledge is nought if it hath not its use for piety, for whereas it neglects to put in practice the good that it knows, it binds itself the more closely to the judgment; and piety is very useless if it lacks the discernment of knowledge, in that while there is no knowledge to enlighten it, it knows not the way to shew mercy. And assuredly unless it has these virtues with it, fear itself rises up to the doing of no good action, forasmuch as while it is agitated about everything, its own alarms render it inactive and void of all good works. Since then by reciprocal ministrations virtue is refreshed by virtue, it is truly said that the sons feast with one another by turns; and as one aids to relieve another, it is as if the numerous offspring to be fed were to prepare a banquet each his day.

It follows; "And sent and called for their three sisters to eat and to drink with them."

When our virtues invite faith, hope, and charity into everything they do, they do as sons employed in labours, call their three sisters to a feast; that faith, hope, and charity may rejoice in the good work which each virtue provides; and they as it were gain strength from that meat, whilst they are rendered more confident by good works.

But what is there that we do in this life, without some stain of defilement, howsoever slight? For sometimes by the very good things we do we draw near to the worse part, since while they beget mirth in the mind, they at the same time engender a certain security, and when the mind enjoys security, it unlooses itself in sloth; and sometimes they defile us with some self-elation, and set us so much the lower with God, as they make us bigger in our own eyes. Hence it is well added, "And it was so, when the days of their feasting were gone about, that Job sent and sanctified them."

For when the round of the days of feasting is gone about, to send to his sons and to sanctify them, is after the perception of the virtues to direct the inward intention, and to purify all that we do with the exact sifting of a re-examination, lest things be counted good which are evil, or at least such as are truly good be thought enough when they are imperfect. For thus it very often happens that the mind is taken in, so that it is deceived either in the quality of what is evil or the quantity of what is good. But these senses of the virtues are much better ascertained by prayers than by examinings.

For the things which we endeavour to search out more completely in ourselves, we oftener obtain a true insight into by praying, than by investigating. For when the mind is lifted up on high by the kind of machine of compunction, all that may have been presented to it concerning itself, it surveys the more surely by passing judgment upon it beneath its feet. Hence it is well subjoined,

"And rose up early in the morning, and offered burnt-offerings, according to the number of them all."

For we rise up early in the morning, when being penetrated with the light of compunction we leave the night of our human state, and open the eyes of the mind to the beams of the true light; and we offer a burnt-offering for each son, when we offer up the sacrifice of prayer for each virtue; lest wisdom may uplift; or understanding, while it runs nimbly, deviate from the right path; or counsel, while it multiplies itself, grow into confusion; that fortitude, while it gives confidence, may not lead to precipitation; lest knowledge, while it knows and yet has no love, may swell the mind; lest piety, while it bends itself out of the right line, may become distorted; and lest fear, while it is unduly alarmed, may plunge one into the pit of despair. When then we pour out our prayers to the Lord in behalf of each several virtue, that it be free from alloy, what else do we but according to the number of our sons offer a burnt-offering for each? for an holocaust is rendered "the whole burnt." Therefore to pay a holocaust is to light up the whole soul with the fire of compunction, that the heart may burn on the altar of love, and consume the defilements of our thoughts, like the sins of our own offspring.

But none know how to do this saving those, who, before their thoughts proceed to deeds, restrain with anxious circumspection the inward motions of their hearts. The entrance to the mind must be fortified with the whole sum of virtue, lest at any time enemies with insidious intent penetrate into it by the opening of heedless thought. Hence Solomon says, "Keep thy heart with all diligence, for out of it are the issues of life." It is meet then that we form a most careful estimate of the virtues that we practise, beginning with the original intent, lest the acts which they put forth, even though they be right, may proceed from a bad origin; and hence it is rightly subjoined,

"For Job said, it may be that my sons have sinned, and cursed God in their hearts."

Our sons curse God in their hearts when our righteous deeds proceed from unrighteous thoughts; when they put forth good things in public, but in secret desire mischief. Thus they curse God when our minds reckon that they get from themselves that which they are. They curse God when they can understand that it is from Him that they have received their powers, and yet seek their own praise for His gifts. But be it known that our old enemy proceeds against our good actions in three ways, with this view namely, that the thing which is done right before the eyes of men, may be spoiled in the sight of the Judge within. For sometimes in a good work he pollutes the intention, that all that follows in the doing may come forth impure and unclean, because it is hereby made to rise troubled from its source. But sometimes he has no power to spoil the intention of a good deed, but he presents himself in the action itself as it were in the pathway; that whereas the person goes forth the more secure in the purpose of his heart, evil being secretly there laid, he may as it were be slain from ambush. And sometimes he neither corrupts the intention, nor overthrows it in the way, but he ensures the good deed at the end of the action; and in proportion as he feigns himself to have gone further off, whether from the house of the heart or from the path of the deed, with the greater craftiness he watches to catch the end of the good action; and the more he has put a man off his guard by seeming to retire, so much the more incurably does he at times pierce him with an unexpected wound.

For he defiles the intention in a good work, in that when he sees men's hearts ready to be deceived, he presents to their ambition the breath of passing applause, that wherein they do aright, they may swerve by crookedness in the intention to make the lowest things their aim.

But when he is unable to corrupt the intention, he conceals snares which he sets in the way, that the heart, lifting itself up in that which is done well, may be impelled from one side to do evil; so that what at the outset it had set before itself in one way, it may go through in act far otherwise than it had begun. For often whilst human praise falls to the lot of a good deed, it alters the mind of the doer; and though not sought after, yet when offered it pleases, and whereas the mind of the well-doer is melted by the delight thereof, it is set loose from all vigorousness of the inward intention. Often when our sense of justice has begun to set aright, anger joins it from the side; and whereas it troubles the mind out of measure, by the quickness of our sense of uprightness, it wounds all the healthiness of our inward tranquillity. It often happens that sadness, attaching itself from the side as it were, becomes the attendant of seriousness of mind, and that every deed which the mind commences with a good intention, this quality overcasts with a veil of sadness, and we are sometimes the slower in driving it away even in that it waits as it were in solemn attendance on the depressed mind. Often immoderate joy attaches itself to a good deed, and while it calls upon the mind for more mirth than is meet, it discards all the weight of gravity from our good actions.

But when our old adversary neither deals a blow at the outset of the intention, nor intercepts us in the path of the execution, he sets the more mischievous snares at the end, which he so much the more wickedly besets, as he sees that it is all that is left to him to make a prey of. Now the Prophet had seen these snares set to the end of his course, when he said, "They will mark my heel." (Ps.

lvi. 6.) Whether then it be evil spirits, or all wicked men that follow in the steps of their pride, they mark the heel when they aim at spoiling the end of a good action, and hence it is said to that serpent, "It shall mark thy head, and thou shalt mark his heel." (Gen. iii. 15. Vulg.) For to mark the serpent's head is to keep an eye upon the beginnings of his suggestions, and with the hand of needful consideration wholly to eradicate them from the avenues of the heart; yet when he is caught at the commencement he busies himself to smite the heel, in that though he does not strike the intention with his suggestion at the first, he strives to ensnare at the end. Now if the heart be once corrupted in the intention, the middle and the end of the action that follows is held in secure possession by the cunning adversary, since he sees that that whole tree bears fruit to himself, which he has poisoned at the root with his hateful tooth. Therefore because we have to watch with the greatest care that the mind even in the service of good works be not polluted by a wicked intention, it is rightly said, "It may be that my sons have sinned, and cursed God in their hearts." As if it were said in plain words, that is no good work which is performed outwardly, unless the sacrifice of innocency be inwardly offered for it upon the altar of the heart in the Presence of God. The stream of our work then is be looked through all we can, if it flows out pure from the wellspring of thought. With all care must the eye of the heart be guarded from the dust of wickedness, lest that which in action it shews upright to man, be within set awry by the fault of a crooked intention.

We must take heed then, that our good works be not too few, take heed that they be not unexamined; lest by doing too few works we be found barren, or by leaving them unexamined we be found foolish; for each several virtue is not really such if it be not blended with other virtues; and hence it is well said to Moses, "Take unto thee sweet spices, stacte, and onycha, and galbanum, of good scent, with pure frankincense; of each there shall be a like weight: and thou shalt make it a perfume, a confection after the art of the apothecary, well tempered together and pure." (Ex. xxx. 34, 35.) For we make a perfume compounded of spices when we yield a smell upon the altar of good works with the multitude of our virtues; and this is tempered together and pure, in that the more we join virtue to virtue, the purer is the incense of good works we set forth. Hence it is well added, "And thou shalt beat them all very small, and put of it before the tabernacle of the testimony." We beat all the spices very small, when we pound our good deeds as it were in the mortar of the heart, by an inward sifting, and go over them minutely, to see if they be really and truly good: and thus to reduce the spices to a powder is to rub fine our virtues by consideration, and to call them back to the utmost exactitude of a secret reviewal; and observe that it is said of that powder, " and thou shalt put of it before the tabernacle of the testimony;" for this reason, in that our good works are then truly pleasing in the sight of our Judge when the mind bruises them small by a more particular re-examination, and as it were makes a powder of the spices, that the good that is done be not coarse and hard, lest if the close hand of re-examination do not bruise it fine, it scatter not from itself the more refined odour. For it is hence that the virtue of the Spouse is commended by the Voice of the Bridegroom, where it is said, "Who is this, that cometh out of the wilderness like a rod of smoke of the perfume of myrrh and frankincense, with all powders of the merchant?" (Cant. iii. 6) For holy Church rises up like a rod of smoke from spices, in that by the virtues of her life she duly advances to the uprightness of inward incense, nor lets herself run out into dissipated thought, but restrains herself in the recesses of the heart by the rod of severity: and while she never ceases to re-consider and go over anew the things that she does, she has in the deed myrrh and frankincense, but in the thought she has powder. Hence it is that it is said again to Moses of those who offer a victim, "And he shall flay the burnt-offering, and cut it into pieces." For we strip the skin of the victim (Levit. i. 6) when we remove from the eyes of the mind the overcast of virtue; and we cut in pieces when we minutely dissect its interior, and contemplate it piecemeal. We must therefore be careful that when we overcome our evil habits, we are not overthrown by our good ones running riot, lest they chance to run out loosely, lest being unheeded they be taken captive, lest from error they forsake the path, lest broken down by weariness they lose the meed of past labours. For the mind ought in all things to keep a wary eye about it, aye and in this very forethought of circumspection to be persevering; and hence it is rightly added,

"Thus did Job all his days." For vain is the good that we do, if it be given over before the end of life, in that it is vain too for him to run fast, who fails before he reaches the goal. For it is hence that it is said of the reprobate, " Woe unto you that have lost patience." (Ecclus. ii. 14.) Hence Truth says to His elect, " Ye are they that have continued with Me in My temptations." (S. Luke xxii. 28.)

Morals of the Book of Job. Bk. i.

Third Sunday in Lent.

THE POOL OF BETHESDA. S. AUG.

WITHOUT doubt it is not without a meaning that these miracles were done, and something they figured out to us bearing on eternal saving health. For the health of body which was restored to the man, of how long duration was it ? " For what is your life ?" saith holy Scripture: " it is a vapour that appeareth for a little time, and then vanisheth away."

Therefore in that health was restored to this man's body for a time, some enduringness was restored to a vapour. So then this is not to be valued much; "Vain is the health of man." And brethren, recollect that prophetical and evangelical testimony, for it is read in the Gospel; "All flesh in grass, and all the glory of flesh as the flower of grass; the grass withereth, the flower falleth away, the Word of the Lord endureth for ever." The Word of the Lord communicateth glory even to the grass, and no transitory glory; for even to flesh He giveth immortality.

But first passeth away the tribulation of this life, out of which he giveth us help, to Whom we have said, "Give us help from tribulation," And all this life is indeed a tribulation to the understanding. For there are two tormentors of the soul, torturing it not at once, but alternating their tortures. These two tormentors' names are Fear and Sorrow. When it is well with thee, thou art in fear; when it is ill, thou art in sorrow. This world's prosperity, whom doth it not deceive, its adversity not break? In this grass, and in the days of grass, the surer way must be kept to, the Word of God. For when it had been said, "All flesh is grass, and all the glory of flesh as the flower of grass, the grass withereth, the flower falleth away;" as though we should ask, "What hope has grass? what stability the flower of grass?" it is said, "but the Word of the Lord endureth for ever." And whence, you will say, is that Word to me? "The Word was made Flesh, and

dwelt among us." For the Word of the Lord was
granted to us, that we might hold to Him, that we
might not pass away with the flower of grass; this
I say, that He hath granted to us, that the Word
should be made Flesh, taking flesh, not changed
into flesh, abiding and assuming; abiding what He
was, assuming what He was not; this I say that
He hath granted to us, that pool also signifies.

I am speaking briefly. That water was the
Jewish people; the five porches were the Law. For
Moses wrote five books. Therefore was the water
inclosed by five porches, as that people was held in
by the Law. The troubling of the water is the
Lord's Passion among that people. He who de-
scended was healed, and only one; for this is unity.
Whosoever are offended at the Passion of Christ are
proud, they will not descend, they are not healed...
To the proud the humiliation of the Lord seems
unworthy of Him, therefore is saving health from
such far off. Lift not thyself up; if thou wouldest
be made whole, descend. Well might piety be
alarmed, if Christ in the flesh subject to change were
only spoken of. But now the truth sets forth to
thee, Christ Unchangable in His Nature as the Word
For, "In the beginning was the Word, and the Word.
was with God;" not a word to sound, and so pass
away; for "the Word was God." So then thy God
endureth unchangeably, O true piety; thy God endureth, fear not; He doth not perish, and through
Him thou too dost not perish. He endureth, He is
born of a woman, but in the flesh. The Word made

I

even His Mother. He Who was before He was made, made her in whom He was to be made Himself. He was an Infant, but in the flesh. He sucked, He grew, He took nourishment, He ran through the several stages of life, He came to man's estate, but in the flesh. He was wearied, and He slept, but in the flesh. He suffered hunger and thirst, but in the flesh. He was apprehended, bound, scourged, assailed with railings, crucified finally, and killed, but in the flesh. Why art thou alarmed? "The Word of the Lord endureth for ever." Whoso rejecteth this humiliation of God, doth not wish for healing from the deadly swelling of pride.

So then by His flesh did the Lord Jesus Christ grant hope to our flesh. For He took on Him what we knew well in this earth, what aboundeth here, to be born and to die. To be born and die abounded here; to rise again and to live for ever was not here. Poor earthly merchandise found He here, He brought here strange and heavenly. If thou art alarmed at death, love the Resurrection. He hath given thee help out of tribulation; for vain thy health had ever been. Let us acknowledge therefore and love the saving health in this world strange, that is, health everlasting, and live we in this world as strangers. Let us think that we are but passing away, so shall we be sinning less. Let us rather give thanks to our Lord God, that He hath been pleased that the last day of this life should be both near and uncertain. From the earliest infancy even to decrepit old age, it is but a short span. If Adam had died to-day, what would it have profited him that he had lived so long? What "long time" is there in that in which there is an end? No one recalleth yesterday; to-day is pressed on by tomorrow, that it may pass away. In this little span let us live well, that we may go whence we may not pass away. And now even as we are talking, we are indeed passing away. Our words run on, and the hours fly by; so does our age, so our actions, so our honours, so our misery, so our happiness here below. All passeth away, but let us not be alarmed; "the Word of God endureth for ever."

Sermons on the New Testament, lxxiv.

Third Monday in Lent.

LOVE AND OBEDIENCE BETTER THAN MIRACLES. S. Chrysostom.

THERE are indeed many things to bind us together. One table is set before all, One Father begat us; we are all the issue of the same throes, the same drink hath been given to all; or rather not only the same drink, but also to drink out of one Cup. For our Father desiring to lead us to a kindly affection, hath desired this also, that we should drink out of one Cup, a thing which belongs to intense love.

"But there is no comparison between the Apostles and us!" I confess it too, and would never deny it. For I say not to themselves, but not even to their shadows are we comparable. But nevertheless let your part be done. This will have no tendency to disgrace you, but rather to profit you the more. For when even to unworthy persons ye shew so much love and obedience, then shall ye receive the greater reward.

We have partaken of a spiritual Table, let us be partakers also of spiritual love. For if robbers on partaking of salt, forget their character, what excuse shall we have, who are continually partaking of the Lord's Body, and do not imitate even their gentleness? And yet to many, not one table only, but even to be of one city, hath sufficed for friendship; but we, when we have the same City, and the same House, and Table, and Day, and Door, and Root, and Life, and Head, and the same Shepherd, and King, and Teacher, and Judge, and Maker, and Father, and to whom all things are common; what indulgence can we deserve, if we be divided one from another?

But the miracles, perhaps, are what ye seek after, such as they wrought when they entered in; the lepers cleansed, the devils driven out, and the dead raised? Nay but this is the great indication of your high birth, and of your love, that ye should believe God without pledges. And in fact this, and one other thing, were the reasons why God made miracles to cease. I mean, that if when miracles are not performed, they that plume themselves on other advantages, for instance either on the word of wisdom, or on show of piety, grow vain-glorious, are puffed up, are separated one from another; did miracles also take place, how could there but be violent rendings? And that what I say is not mere conjecture, the Corinthians bear witness, who from this cause were divided into many parties.

Do not thou therefore seek signs, but the soul's health. Seek not to see one dead man raised; nay, for thou hast learnt that the whole world is arising. Seek not to see a blind man healed, but behold all now restored unto that better and more profitable sight; and do thou too learn to look chastely, and amend thine eye. For in truth, if we all lived as we ought, workers of miracles would not be admired so much as we by the children of the heathen. For as to the signs, they often carry with them either a notion of mere fancy, or another evil suspicion, although ours be not such. But a pure life cannot admit of any such reproach; yea, all men's mouths are stopped by the acquisition of virtue.

Let virtue then be our study; for abundant are her riches, and great the wonder wrought in her. She bestows the true freedom, and causes the same to be discerned even in slavery, not releasing from slavery, but while men continue slaves, exhibiting them more honourable than freemen; which is much more than giving them freedom; not making the poor man rich, but while he continues poor, exhibiting him wealthier than the rich.

But if thou wouldest work miracles also, be rid of transgressions, and thou hast quite accomplished it. Yea, for sin is a great demon, beloved; and if thou exterminate this, thou hast wrought a greater thing than they who drive out ten thousand demons. Do thou listen to Paul, how he speaks, and prefers virtue to miracles. "But covet earnestly," saith he, "the best gifts; and yet shew I unto you a more excellent way." (1 Cor. xii. 31.) And when he was to declare this "way," he spake not of raising the dead, not of cleansing the lepers, nor of any such thing; but in place of all these he set charity. Listen also unto Christ, saying, "Rejoice not that the demons obey you, but that your names are written in heaven." (S. Luke x. 20.) And again before this, "Many will say to Me in that day, Have we not prophesied in Thy Name, and cast out devils, and done many mighty works? And then I will profess unto you, I know you not." And when He was about to be crucified, He called His disciples, and said unto them, "By this shall all men know that ye are My disciples," not, "if ye cast out devils," but "if ye have love one to another." And again, "Hereby shall all men know that Thou hast sent Me;" not "if these men raise the dead," but "if they be one."

For as to miracles, they oftentimes while they profited another, injured him who had the power, by lifting him up to pride and vain-glory, or haply in some other way, but in our works there is no place for any such suspicion, but they profit both such as follow them, and many others.

These then let us perform with much diligence. For if thou change from inhumanity to almsgiving, thou hast stretched forth the hand that was withered. If thou withdraw from theatres and go to the church, thou hast cured the lame foot. If thou draw back thine eyes from unholy gazing, thou hast opened them when they were blind. If instead of satanical songs thou hast learnt spiritual psalms, being dumb thou hast spoken.

These are the greatest miracles, these the wonderful signs. If we go on working these signs, we shall both ourselves be a great and admirable sort of persons through these, and shall win over all the wicked unto virtue; and shall enjoy the life to come; unto which may we all attain, by the grace and love towards man of our Lord Jesus Christ, to whom be glory and might for ever and ever. Amen.

Homil. in S. Matt. xxxii.

Third Tuesday in Lent.

MEEKNESS. S. CHRYSOSTOM.

LET us not stop at calling the beloved Disciple blessed, but let us do all things that we also may be of the blessed; let us imitate the Evangelist, and see what it was that caused such great love. What then was it? He left his father, his ship, and his net, and followed Jesus. Yet this did he in common with his brother, and Peter, and Andrew, and the rest of the Apostles. What then was the special thing which caused this great love? Shall we discover it? He saith nothing of this kind about himself, but only that he was beloved; as to the righteous acts for which he was beloved he has modestly been silent. That Jesus loved him with an especial love was clear to every one; yet John doth not appear conversing with or questioning Jesus privately, as Peter often did, and Philip, and Thomas, except only when he desired to shew kindness and compliance to his fellow Apostle; for when the chief of the Apostles by beckoning constrained him, then he asked, for these two had great love each for the other. Thus, for instance, they are seen going up together into the temple and speaking in common to the people. Yet Peter in many places is moved, and speaks more warmly than John. And at the end he hears Christ say, "Peter, lovest thou Me more than these?" Now it is clear that he who loved "more than these" was also beloved. But this in his case was shewn by loving Jesus, in the case of the other by being beloved by Jesus.

What then was it which caused this especial love? To my thinking it was that the man displayed great gentleness and meekness, for which reason he doth not appear in many places speaking openly. And how great a thing this is, is plain also from the case of Moses. It is this which made him such and so great as he was. There is nothing equal to lowliness of mind. For which cause. Jesus with this began the Beatitudes, and when about to lay as it were the foundation and base of a mighty building, He placed first lowliness of mind. Without this a man cannot possibly be saved, though he fast, though he pray, though he give alms, if it be with a proud spirit; these things are abominable, if humility be not there; while if it be, all these things are amiable and lovely, and are done with safety. Let us then be modest, beloved, let us be modest; success is easy, if we be sober-minded. For after all what is it, O man, that exciteth thee to pride? Seest thou not the poverty of thy nature? the unsteadiness of thy will? Consider thine end, consider the multitude of thy sins. But perhaps because thou doest many righteous deeds thou art proud? By that very pride thou shalt undo them all. Wherefore it behoveth not so much him that has sinned as him that doth righteousness to take pains to be humble. Why so? Because the sinner is constrained by conscience, while the other, except he be very sober, is soon caught up as by a blast of wind, is lifted on high, and made to vanish like the Pharisee. Dost thou give to the poor? What thou givest is not thine, but thy Master's, common to thee and thy fellow servants. For which cause thou oughtest especially to be humbled in the calamities of those who are thy kindred, foreseeing thine own, and taking knowledge of thine own nature in their cases. We ourselves perhaps are sprung from such ancestors, and if wealth has shifted to you, it is probable that it will leave you again. And after all, what is wealth? A vain shadow, dissolving smoke, a flower of the grass, or rather something meaner than a flower. Or dost thou desire honour? Towards gaining honour nothing is more serviceable than almsgiving. For the honours arising from wealth and power are compulsory, and attended with hatred, but these others are from the free will and real feeling of the honourers; and therefore those who pay them can never give them up. Now if men shew such reverence for the merciful, and invoke all blessings upon them, consider what return, what recompense they shall receive from the merciful God. Let us then seek this wealth which endureth for ever, and never deserts us, that, becoming great here and glorious there, we may obtain everlasting blessings, through the grace and lovingkindness of our Lord Jesus Christ, with Whom, &c.

In S. John. Homil. xxxii.

Fourth Wednesday in Lent.

TAKING UP THE CROSS. S. AUGUSTINE.

HARD and grievous does that appear which the Lord hath enjoined, that "whosoever will come after Him, must deny himself." But what He enjoineth is not hard or grievous, Who aideth us that what He enjoineth may be done. For both is that true which is said to Him in the Psalm, "Because of the words of Thy Lips I have kept hard ways" (Ps. xvi. 4. Sept.): and that is true which He said Himself, "My yoke is easy, and My burden is light." For whatsoever is hard in what is enjoined us, love makes easy. We know what great things love itself can do. Very often is this love even abominable and impure; but how great hardships have men suffered, what indignities and intolerable things have they endured, to attain to the object of their love? whether it be a lover of money, who is called covetous, or a lover of honour, who is called ambitious, or any other lover. Consider what labour all lovers undergo, and are not conscious of their labours; and then does any such one most feel labour, when he is hindered from it. Since then the majority of men are such as their loves are, and that there ought to be no other care for the regulation of our lives than the choice of that which we ought to love, why dost thou wonder if he who loves Christ, and who wishes to follow Christ, for the love of Him denies himself? For if by loving himself man is lost, surely by denying himself he is found.

The first destruction of man was the love of himself. For if he had not loved himself, if he had preferred God to himself, he would have been willing to be ever subject unto God, and would not have been turned to the neglect of His Will and the doing his own will. For this is to love one's-self, to wish to do one's own will. Prefer to this God's Will; learn to love thyself by not loving thyself. For that ye may know that it is a vice to love one's-self, the Apostle speaks thus, "Men shall be lovers of their own selves." And can he who loves himself have any sure trust in himself? No; for he begins to love himself by forsaking God, and is driven away from himself to love those things which are beyond himself, to such a degree that when the aforesaid Apostle had said, "Men shall be lovers of their own selves," he subjoined immediately, "lovers of money." Already thou seest that thou art without; thou hast begun to love thyself, stand in thyself if thou canst. Thou hast begun to love what is without thee, thou hast lost thyself. When a man's love goes even away from those things which are without, he begins to share the vanity of his vain desires, and prodigal as it were to spend his strength. He is dissipated, exhausted, without resource or strength, he feeds swine, and wearied with this office, he at last remembers what he was, and says, "How many hired servants of my father's are eating bread, and I here perish with hunger!"

But when "he returned to himself" he said, "I will arise and go to my father." See whence he had fallen away from himself, he had fallen away from his father; he had fallen from himself, he had gone away from himself to those things which are without. He returns to himself, and goes to his father, where he may keep himself in all security. If then he had gone away from himself, let him also in returning to himself, from whom he had gone away, that he may "go to his father," deny himself. What is "deny himself?" let him not trust in himself, let him feel that he is a man, and have respect unto the words of the prophet, "Cursed is every one that putteth his hope in man." Let him withdraw from himself, not towards things below, but that he may cleave to God. Whatever of good he has, let him commit it to Him by Whom he was made; whatever of evil he has, he has made it for himself. The evil that is in him God made not; let him destroy what himself has done, who has been thereby undone. "Let him deny himself," He saith, "and take up his cross, and follow Me."

And whither must the Lord be followed? He has ascended into heaven. Thither must He be followed. Undoubtedly we must not despair of it, because He hath Himself promised us, not because man can do anything. Heaven was far away from us, before that our Head had gone into heaven. But now why should we despair, if we are members of that Head? Thither then must He be followed. And who would be unwilling to follow Him to such an abode? especially seeing that we are in so great travail on earth with fears and pains. Who would be unwilling to follow Christ thither, where is supreme felicity, supreme peace, perpetual security? Good is it to follow Him thither; but we must see by what way we are to follow. For the Lord Jesus did not say these words after He had risen from the dead. He had not yet suffered, He had still to come to the Cross, had to come to His dishonouring, to the outrages, the scourging, the thorns, the wounds, the mockeries, the insults, death. Rough as it were is the way; it makes thee to be slow; thou hast no mind to follow. But follow on. Rough is the way which man has made for himself, but what Christ hath trodden in His passage is worn smooth. For who would not wish to go to exaltation? Elevation is pleasing to all; but humility is the step to it. Why dost thou put out thy foot beyond thee? Thou hast a mind to fall, not to ascend. Begin by the step, and so thou hast ascended. This step of humility those two disciples were loth to have an eye to who said, "Lord, bid that one of us may sit at Thy right Hand, and the other at Thy left in Thy kingdom." They sought for exaltation, they did not see the step. But the Lord shewed them the step. For what did He answer them? Ye who seek the will of exaltation, can ye drink the cup of humiliation? And therefore He does not say simply, let him deny himself, and follow Me howsoever: but He said more, "Let him take up his cross and follow Me." What is, "Let him take up his cross?" Let him bear whatever trouble he has; so let him follow Me. For when he shall begin to follow Me in conformity to My life and precepts, he will have many to contradict him, he will have many to hinder him; he will have many to dissuade him, and that from among those who are even as it were Christ's companions. They who hindered the blind man from crying out were walking with Christ. Whether therefore they be threats or caresses, or whatsoever hindrances there be, if thou wish to follow, turn them into thy cross, bear it, carry it, do not give way beneath it. There seems to be an exhortation to martyrdom in these words of the Lord. If there be persecution, ought not all things to be despised in consideration of Christ? The world is loved; but let Him be preferred by Whom the world was made. Great is the world; but greater is He by Whom the world was made. Fair is the world; but fairer is He by Whom the world was made. Sweet is the world, but sweeter is He by Whom the world was made. Evil is the world; and good is He by Whom the world was made.

To whatever point then, any one has been able to reach, let him fear to " look back " from thence ; and let him walk in the way, let him " follow Christ." " Forgetting those things which are behind, and stretching forth unto those things which are before, let him by an earnest inward intention press on toward the prize of the calling of God in Christ Jesus."

Homil. on the New Test., xlvi.

Fourth Thursday in Lent.

UNITY OF THE CHURCH. S. CYPRIAN.

OUR Lord Jesus Christ when He testified in the Gospel that they were His adversaries who were " not with " Him, did not designate any species of heresy, but shewed that all whatsoever who " were not with Him," and who "gathering not with Him, scattered" His flock, were His adversaries; saying, "He that is not with Me is against Me, and he that gathereth not with Me scattereth." So neither did the blessed Apostle John distinguish any one heresy or schism, or set down that any were specially separated, but all who had gone out of the Church, and who acted against the Church, he called antichrists, saying, "Ye have heard that antichrist shall come, and now are come many antichrists. Wherefore we know that it is the last time. They went out from us, but they were not of us; for if they had been of us, they would have continued with us." Whence it appears that all are adversaries of the Lord and antichrists, who are found to have departed from the charity and unity of the Catholic Church. Moreover the Lord in His Gospel lays it down, and says, "But if he neglect to hear the Church let him be unto thee as an heathen man and a publican." But if they who despise the Church are accounted heathens and publicans, much more surely must rebels and enemies, who invent false altars and unlawful priesthoods and sacrilegious sacrifices and spurious names, needs be reckoned among heathens and publicans, since they who sin less and but neglect the Church are by the sentence of the Lord adjudged to be heathens and publicans.

But that the Church is one, the Holy Ghost declares in the Song of Solomon; saying in the Person of Christ, "My dove, My undefiled is one; she is the only one of her Mother, she is the choice one of her that bare her." Of whom also He saith in another place, "A garden inclosed is My sister, My spouse: a spring sealed up, a well of living water." But if the "spouse" of Christ, which is the Church, "is a garden inclosed," a thing closed cannot lie open to aliens and the profane. And if it is a "spring sealed up," we can neither drink thence, nor be sealed [1], who being placed without have not access to the spring. The "well" too of "living water," if it is one and also within, whoso is placed without cannot be enlivened and sanctified with that water, which they only who are within are permitted to use and drink. This also Peter, shewing that the Church is one, and that they only who are in the Church can be baptized, laid down, saying, "In the ark of Noah few, that is, eight souls, were saved by water, the like figure whereunto even Baptism shall save you;" proving and testifying that the one ark of Noah was a type of the one Church. If then in that Baptism of the cleansed and purified world, he could be "saved by water" who was not in the ark of Noah; now also he may be enlivened by Baptism who is not in the Church to which alone Baptism has been granted.

Moreover the Apostle Paul, declaring this same thing more expressly and clearly, writes to the Ephesians, and says, "Christ loved the Church and gave Himself for it, that He might sanctify, and cleanse it with the washing of water." But if the Church which is loved by Christ is one, and which

[1] With the seal of Baptism.

alone is cleansed by His washing, how can he that is not in the Church either be loved by Christ or be washed and cleansed by His washing?

The Lord, intimating to us that unity cometh of Divine authority, declareth and saith, "I and My Father are One." To which unity bringing His Church He further saith, "There shall be one fold, and one Shepherd." But if there is "one flock," how can he be numbered as of the flock who is not in the number of the flock? or how he accounted a shepherd, who, the true shepherd remaining and by successive ordination presiding in the Church of God, himself, succeeding to no one and beginning from himself, becomes an alien and profane, an enemy to the Lord's peace, and to the Divine unity; not dwelling in the house of God, that is, in the Church of God, in which they only dwell who are of one heart and one mind? for that the Holy Ghost speaks in the Psalms and says, "He is the God that maketh men to be of one mind in an house." Moreover even the very sacrifices of the Lord do shew Christian unanimity knit together, by form and inseparate charity. For when the Lord calls bread, which is made up of the union of many grains, His Body, He indicates one people whom He bore, united together; and when He calls wine which is pressed from many bunches and clusters, and drawn into one, His Blood, He likewise signifies one flock joined together by the mingling of an united multitude.

Moreover, how inseparable the sacrament of unity is, and how without hope they are, and what exceeding perdition they purchase to themselves from the wrath of God, who make a schism, and abandoning their bishop set up for themselves another false bishop without, holy Scripture declares in the Book of Kings, when ten tribes severed from the tribe of Judah and Benjamin, and abandoning their king, set up another for themselves without. "The Lord," it saith, "was very angry with all the seed of Israel, and removed them away, and delivered them into the hand of spoilers, until He had cast them out of His sight; for Israel was rent from the house of David, and they made themselves a king, Jeroboam the son of Nebat." It is said that "the Lord was very angry," and gave them up to perdition, because they were separated from unity, and had set up for themselves another king. And so great was the anger of the Lord against those who had caused the schism, that even when the man of God was sent to Jeroboam to reproach him for his sins, and to foretell the vengeance that would follow, he was forbidden "to eat bread or drink water" with them; which when he did not observe, and against the command of God took food, he was immediately stricken by the majesty of the Divine judgment, so that returning thence he was slain in the way by the jaws of a lion who came against him. And does any one dare to say that the saving water of Baptism and heavenly grace can be in common with schismatics, with whom neither earthly food nor this world's drink ought to be in common?

Epist. lxix. ad Magnus.

Fourth Friday in Lent.

CONFESSION OF SINS. S. AUGUSTINE.

WHAT he can, let man do, let him confess himself what he is, that he may be cured by Him Who always is what He is: for He always was and is; we were not and are.

For see what He saith: "If we say that we have no sin we deceive ourselves, and the truth is not in us." Consequently if thou have confessed thyself a sinner, the truth is in thee: for the Truth Itself is Light. Thy life hath not yet shone in perfect brightness, because there are sins in thee; but yet thou hast already begun to be enlightened, because there is in thee the confession of sins. For see what follows: "If we confess our sins, He is faithful and just to forgive us our sins, and to purge us from all iniquity." Not only the past, (original sin,) but haply if we have contracted any from this life; because a man, so long as he bears the flesh, cannot but have some at any rate light sins. But these which we call light do not thou make light of. If thou make light of them when thou weighest them, be afraid when thou countest them. Many light make one huge sin: many drops fill the river: many grains make the lump. And what hope is there? Before all, confession: lest any think himself righteous, and before the Eyes of God Who seeth that which is, man, which was not and is, lift up the neck. Before all then, confession; then love; for of charity what is said? "Charity covereth a multitude of sins." Now let us see whether he commendeth charity in regard of the sins which subsequently overtake us; because charity alone extinguisheth sins. Pride extinguisheth charity: therefore humility strengtheneth charity; charity extinguisheth sins. Humility goes along with confession, the humility by which we confess ourselves sinners; this is humility, not to say it with the tongue, as if only to avoid arrogancy, lest we should displease men should we say that we are righteous. This do the ungodly and insane: "I know indeed that I am righteous, but what shall I say before men? If I shall call myself righteous, who will hear it, who tolerate? let my righteousness be known unto God: I however will say that I am a sinner, but only that I be not found odious for arrogancy." Tell man what thou art, tell God what thou art. Because if thou tell not God what thou art, God condemneth what He shall find in thee. Wouldest thou not that He condemn thee? Condemn thou. Wouldest thou that He forgive? Do thou acknowledge, that thou mayest be able to say unto God, "Turn Thy face from my sins." Say also to Him those words in the same Psalm, "For I acknowledge mine iniquity." "If we confess our sins, He is faithful and just to forgive us our sins, and to purge us from all iniquity." "If we say that we have not sinned, we make Him a liar, and His

Word is not in us." If thou shalt say, I have not sinned, thou makest Him a liar, while thou wishest to make thyself true. How is it possible that God should be a liar and men true, when the Scripture saith the contrary, "Every man a liar, God Alone true?" Consequently, God true through Himself, thou true through God, became through thyself a liar.

And lest haply the Apostle should seem to have given impunity for sins, in that he said, "He is faithful and just to cleanse us from all iniquity;" and men henceforth should say to themselves, Let us sin, let us do securely what we will, Christ purgeth us, He is faithful and just, purgeth us from all iniquity: He taketh from thee an evil security, and putteth in an useful fear. To thine own hurt thou wouldest be secure; thou must be solicitous. For "He is faithful and just to forgive us our faults," provided thou always displease thyself, and be changing until thou be perfected. Accordingly, what follows? "My little children, these things I write unto you, that ye sin not." But perchance sin overtakes us from our mortal life: what shall be done then? What? shall there be now despair? Hear: "And if any man sin, we have an Advocate with the Father, Jesus Christ the Righteous; and He is the propitiation for our sins." He then is the Advocate, do thou endeavour not to sin; if from the infirmity of this life sin shall overtake thee, see to it straightway, straightway be displeased, straightway condemn it; and when thou hast condemned, thou shalt come assured unto the

Judge. There hast thou the Advocate: fear not to lose thy cause in thy confession. For if oft-times in this life a man commits his cause to an eloquent tongue, and is not lost: thou committest thyself to the Word, and shalt thou be lost? Cry, "We have an Advocate with the Father."

Homil. on S. John, Epist. i.

Fourth Saturday in Lent.

ANGER. S. CHRYSOSTOM.

IT is impossible for one out of temper to accomplish his purpose, and persuade any; he must make him to whom he speaks still more incredulous. Wherefore we must abstain from anger, and make our words in every way credible by avoiding not only wrath, but also loud speaking, for loud speaking is the fuel of passion.

Let us then bind the horse, that we may subdue the rider; let us clip the wings of our wrath, so the evil shall no more rise to a height. A keen passion is anger; keen and skilful to steal our souls; therefore we must on all sides guard against its entrance. It were strange that we should be able to tame wild beasts, and yet should neglect our own savage minds. Wrath is a fierce fire, it devours all things; it harms the body, it destroys the soul, it makes a man deformed and ugly to look upon, and if it were possible for an angry person to be visible to himself at the time of his anger, he would need no other admonition, for nothing is more displeasing than an angry countenance. Anger is a kind of drunkenness, or rather it is more grievous than drunkenness, and more pitiable than possession of a demon. It has overturned whole houses, it has dissolved old companionships, and has worked tragedies not to be remedied in a short moment of time. Let us then be careful not to be loud in speech, we shall find this the best path to sobriety of conduct. And therefore Paul would take away clamour as well as anger, when he says, "Let all anger and clamour be put away from you." Let us then obey this teacher of all wisdom, and whenever a friend grieves thee, or one of thine own family exasperates thee, think of the sins thou hast committed against God, and that by kindness towards him thou makest that judgment more lenient to thyself, ("Forgive," saith He, "and ye shall be forgiven,") and thy passion shall quickly skulk away. And besides, consider this, whether there has been a time when thou wert being carried away into ferocity, and didst control thyself, and another time when thou hast been dragged along by the passion. Compare the two seasons, and thou shalt gain great improvement. For tell me, when didst thou praise thyself? Was it when thou wast worsted, or when thou hadst the mastery? Do we not in the first case vehemently blame ourselves, and feel ashamed even when none reproves us? And do not many feelings of repentance come over us, both for what we have said and done; but when we gain the mastery, then are we not proud, and exult as conquerors? For victory in the case of anger is, not the requiting evil with the like, (that is utter defeat,) but the bearing meekly to be ill treated and ill spoken of. To get the better is not to inflict but to suffer evil. Therefore when angry do not say, "Certainly I will retaliate," or "Certainly I will be revenged." Look up straight to God, He will praise thee, and the man who is approved by Him must not seek honour from mortals. Think when thou art angry that it is God Himself Who bids thee be silent, and then thou wilt bear all things meekly and say to the aggressor, "How can I be angry with thee? there is another that restrains both my hand and my tongue;" and the saying will be a suggestion of sound wisdom, both to thyself and to him. Considering then all these things, and calling to mind our own transgressions, and the common nature of man, let us be careful at all times to speak gently, that being humble in heart we may find rest for our souls, both that which now is, and that which is to come, which may we all attain, by the grace and loving-kindness of our Lord Jesus Christ, to Whom, &c.

In S. Johan. Hom. xxvi. and iv.

Fourth Sunday in Lent.

RIGHT USE OF LENT, FORGIVENESS OF INJURIES. S. Chrysostom.

At length the season is verging towards the end of the fast, and therefore we ought the more earnestly to devote ourselves to holiness. For as in the case of those who run a race, all their circuits will be of no avail if they fall short of the prize; so neither will any advantage result from these manifold labours and toils with regard to the fast, if we are not able to enjoy the sacred Table with a good conscience. For this end are fasting and Lent appointed, and so many days of solemn assemblies, auditories, prayers, and teaching, in order that by this earnestness being cleansed in every possible way from the sins which we had contracted during the whole year, we may with spiritual boldness religiously partake of that unbloody sacrifice; so that should this not be the result, we shall have sustained so much labour entirely in vain and without any profit. Let every one therefore consider with himself what defect he hath corrected, what good work he hath attained to; what sin he hath cast off, what stain he hath purged away; wherein he hath become better. And should he discover that in this good traffic he hath made any gain by the fast, and be conscious in himself of much care taken of his wounds, let him draw near. But if he hath remained in neglect, having nothing to shew but mere fasting, and hath done nothing which is right besides, let him remain without; and then let him enter, when he hath purged out all these offences. Let no one rest on the fast merely, whilst remaining unreformed from evil practices. For it is probable that he who omits fasting may obtain pardon, having infirmity of body to plead; but it is impossible that he can have one excuse who hath not amended his faults. Thou hast not fasted it may be, on account of bodily weakness. Tell me for what reason thou art not reconciled to thine enemies? Hast thou indeed here to allege bodily infirmity? Again; if thou retainest envy and hatred, what apology hast thou then I ask? For no one in offences of this kind is able to take refuge in the plea of bodily infirmity. And this was a work of Christ's love towards man, i. e. that the chief of the precepts, and those which maintain our life, should not be susceptible of any kind of interference through the weakness of the body.

But since we need to practise all the divine laws alike, and more especially that which bids us consider no man as an enemy, nor retain resentment long, but forthwith to be reconciled; suffer us to-day to discourse to you concerning this commandment. For as it is not imagined that the fornicator and the blasphemer can partake of the sacred Table, so it is impossible that he who hath an enemy, and bears malice, can enjoy the Holy Communion... How canst thou ask the Lord to be mild and merciful to thee when thou art hard and unforgiving to thy fellow-servant?

But thy fellow-servant hath treated thee with contempt perhaps? Yes! and thou hast treated God with contempt oftentimes. And what comparison is there between a fellow-servant and the Lord? As to the former, when he was perchance in some way injured, he insulted thee, and thou wast exasperated. But thou insultest the Lord, when thou art neither treated with injustice nor ill-will by Him, but receiving blessings of Him each day. Consider then, that if God chose to search out rigorously what is done against Him, we should not live a single day. For the prophet saith, "If Thou wilt be extreme to mark iniquity, O Lord, who shall stand?" And to pass by all those other things, of which the conscience of every sinner is aware, and which have no human witness, but God only, were we to be called to account for those which are open and admitted, what allowance could we expect for such sins? What if a close examination were made into our listlessness and negligence in our prayers; how that whilst standing before God and supplicating Him, we do not exhibit even so much fear and reverence for Him as servants do towards their masters, as soldiers do towards their officers, as friends do towards friends? When thou discoursest with a friend, thou givest heed to what thou art doing, but when waiting on God on account of thy sins, and asking pardon for so many offences, and thinking

that thou shalt obtain forgiveness, thou art often
listless; and whilst thy knees are on the ground,
thou sufferest thy mind to wander every where; in
the market or in the house, babbling the while with
thy mouth vainly and to no purpose. And this we
allow to be so, not once or twice, but frequently!
Did God then choose rigorously to search into this
alone, do you think that we could obtain pardon,
or be able to advance any excuse? Truly I think
not.

But what if the evil speakings which we unkindly
utter every day one against another were brought
forward against us; as well as the rash judgment
with which we condemn our neighbour; and that
for no reason, but because we are fond of blaming,
and given to find fault; what I say should we be able
to allege in defence? Again should He rigorously
examine those roving glances of ours, and those evil
desires which we carry in the mind, so frequently
admitting impure and disgraceful thoughts, what
punishment must we not sustain? And should He
demand a reason for our revilings, (for He saith,
"Whosoever shall say to his brother, Thou fool, shall
be in danger of hell fire?") how could we forsooth
open our mouths, or move our lips at all, or say
any thing great or small in reply? Moreover as to
the vainglorious feelings we allow in our prayers, our
fastings, our almsgivings, were we to search rigorously into them, I do not say, were God, but were
we ourselves, who are the sinners, to do this, should
we be able to lift up our eyes toward heaven? Then,

as to the deceits which we devise one against another, praising a brother now whilst he is present, and discoursing as with a friend; and when he is absent reviling him; can we endure the punishments of all these? Then what of the oaths? or what of the lying? what of the perjuries? what of the unjust anger, and of the envy with which we too often regard men when honoured, who are not enemies but friends? Furthermore, what of the fact that we are pleased when others suffer evil, and account the misfortunes of others a consolation for our own distress?

But suppose the penalty were exacted for our listlessness in our solemn assemblies? Do not suppose that this offence is a small one, yet God is thus treated by us with great contempt, and is still forbearing and longsuffering, not in regard to this alone, but to other things which are far more grievous. For these things are what must be admitted, and what are obvious to all, and by almost all men they are daringly practised. But there are yet others, which the conscience of those who commit them is privy to. Surely, if we were to think of all this; if we were to reason with ourselves, supposing even that we were insensible and obdurate in the worst degree, yet upon taking a survey of the multitude of our sins, we should for very fear and agony be unable to remember the injury done by others toward themselves. Bear in mind the river of fire; the envenomed worm; the fearful judgment, where all things shall be naked and open? Reflect, that what are now hidden things, are then to be brought to light! But shouldest thou pardon thy neighbours, all these sins which till then await their disclosure are done away with here; and thou wilt depart this life dragging after thee none of that chain of transgressions; so that thou receivest greater things than thou givest. For many such transgressions, indeed, we have often committed which no other person knoweth; and when we think that on that day when our sins shall lie exposed to the eyes of all upon the public theatre of the universe, we are in pain beyond any punishment, whilst choked and strangled by our conscience. Yet this shame, great as it is, these sins, these punishments, great as they are, there is a possibility of purging away through forgiveness exercised toward our neighbour.

God continually exhorts us saying, "Let none of you revengefully imagine evil against his brother in your heart, and let none of you think of his neighbour's malice." (Zech. vii. and viii.) It is not said merely, forego wrath, but retain it not in thy mind; think not of it, part with all thy resentment. Do away the sore; for thou supposest that thou art paying him back the injury, but thou art first tormenting thyself, and setting up thy rage as an executioner within thee in every part, tearing up thine own bounds. For what can be more wretched than a man continually provoked?

"Rejoice not," the Wise man saith, "when thine enemy stumbleth." (Prov. xxiv. 17.) And tell me not of the greatness of the injuries received; for it is not this which maketh thy wrath to be retained; but this, that thou art unmindful of thine own offences; that thou hast not before thine eyes either hell or the fear of God.

Neither infirmity of body, nor poverty, nor unlettered ignorance, nor want of leisure, nor any other thing of that kind hast thou to advance. How wilt thou be able to stretch thine hands towards heaven, or how to move thy tongue, or to ask pardon? For although God be desirous to pardon thy sins, thou thyself dost not suffer Him, while thou retainest that of thy fellow servant! But suppose that he is cruel, fierce and savage, and greedy of revenge and retaliation? Why for this reason thou oughtest especially to grant forgiveness. Hast thou been wronged much, and robbed, and slandered, and injured in matters of first importance; and dost thou wish to see thine enemy punished? Yet if thou thyself takest vengeance, and prosecutest it, either by words, by deeds, or imprecation against the adversary; then God will not afterwards prosecute it too, inasmuch as thou hast taken thy revenge; and not only will He not prosecute the matter for thee, but will also demand a penalty of thee, as a despiser of Himself.

Hath thy neighbour wronged and grieved thee, and involved thee in a thousand ills? Be it so, yet do not prosecute vengeance on thine own part, lest thou be treating thy Lord with contempt! Yield the matter to God, and He will dispose of it much better than thou canst desire. To thee He has given charge simply to pray for the injurer; but how to deal with him, He hath ordered thee to leave to Himself. Never canst thou so avenge thyself, as He is prepared to avenge thee, if thou givest place to Him alone.

Lo! I forewarn, and testify, and proclaim this with a voice that all may hear! Let no one who hath an enemy approach the sacred Table, or receive the Lord's Body. Let no one approaching have an enemy. Hast thou an enemy? Approach not! Wilt thou approach? Be reconciled and then approach, and touch the holy Thing.

Nor indeed is this my declaration: rather it is that of the Lord Himself, Who was crucified for us. That He might reconcile thee to the Father, He refused not to be slaughtered, and to shed His Blood. And art thou unwilling to utter a word, or to make the first advance, that thou mayest be reconciled to thy fellow servant? Hear what the Lord saith, "If thou bring thy gift to the altar, and there rememberest that thy brother hath aught against thee." He does not say, "wait for him to come to thee;" nor "speak with another as a mediator," but "do thou thyself make the advance towards him."

We are commanded to have only one enemy, the devil. With him never be thou reconciled. But with a brother, never have a heart at enmity! For when thou sayest, "Forgive us as we forgive," and afterwards dost not forgive, thou art supplicating of God nothing else than that He would entirely deprive thee of all excuse or indulgence. No one so truly pollutes the holy Feast, as he does, who while

L

he is keeping it, cherishes malignity. Where there is strife and enmity there can be neither fast nor festival. Thou wouldest not dare to touch the holy Sacrifice with unwashed hands: approach not then with an unwashed soul! For this is far more than the other, and brings a heavier punishment. Nothing so fills the mind with impurity as anger remaining constantly within it. The Spirit of meekness hovers not where wrath or passion exists; and when a man is destitute of the Holy Spirit, what hope of salvation shall he have, and how shall he walk upright?

Had it been an evil thing to suffer wrong, God would not have enjoined it upon us. Know ye not that He is the King of Glory, and therefore He commands us to suffer wrong, and doth all to withdraw us from worldly things, and to convince us what is glory, and what shame; what loss, and what gain. Say you, "I have been shamefully used, and do you exhort me to bear it meekly? How shall I be able?" Nay but it is most easy, if thou wilt look up unto heaven; if thou wilt behold the beauty that is in sight; and whither God hath promised to receive thee, if thou bear wrong nobly. Do this then, and looking up unto the heaven, think that thou art made like unto Him that sitteth there upon the cherubim. For He also was (as at this time) injured and bore it; He was reproached and avenged not Himself; and was spit upon, yet He asserted not His cause. Nay, He made return, in the contrary kind, to those who did such things, even in benefits without number; and He hath commanded us to be imitators of Him.

Wouldst thou desire to know in earnest how great are the blessings which await thee? He openeth for thee the whole heaven; He maketh thee a fellow citizen with the saints; He fits thee to bear a part in their choir: from sins He absolveth, with righteousness He crowneth. For if such as forgive offenders shall obtain forgiveness, those who not only forgive but who also give largely to boot, what blessing shall they not inherit! Therefore pray for him that injured thee. It is for thyself that thou dost this. Hath he taken thy money? Well: he took thy sins too; which was the case with Naaman and Gehazi. How much wealth wouldest thou not give, to have thine iniquities forgiven thee? This, believe me, is the case now. For if thou endure nobly and curse not, thou hast bound on thee a glorious crown. It is not my word; but thou hast heard Christ speaking. "Pray for those that despitefully use you." And consider the reward how great! "That ye may be like your Father which is in the heavens."

Let us not then be negligent of what is our life, but let us be in earnest, and do every thing in order that we may be without an enemy to present ourselves at the sacred Table, for nothing, I repeat, of what God commands will be difficult, if we give heed.

De Stat. Hom. xx., and Hom. in 1 Cor. xvi.

Fourth Monday in Lent.

CHRIST ASLEEP IN THE STORM. S. Aug.

This sleep of Christ is the sign of a high mystery. The sailors are the souls passing over the world in wood. That ship also was a figure of the Church. And all individually indeed are temples of God, and his own heart is the vessel in which each sails; nor can he suffer shipwreck, if his thoughts are only good.

Thou hast heard an insult, it is the wind; thou art angry, it is a wave. When therefore the wind blows, and the wave swells, the ship is endangered, the heart is in jeopardy, the heart is tossed to and fro.

When thou hast heard an insult, thou longest to be avenged; and lo, avenged thou hast been, and so rejoicing in another's harm thou hast suffered shipwreck. And why is this? Because Christ is asleep in thee. What does this mean, Christ is asleep in thee? Thou hast forgotten Christ. Rouse Him up then, call Christ to mind, let Christ awake in thee, give heed to Him. What didst thou wish? To be avenged. Hast thou forgotten that when He was being crucified, He said, "Father, forgive them, for they know not what they do?" He who was asleep in thy heart did not wish to be avenged. Awake Him up then, call Him to remembrance. The remembrance of Him is His command. And then wilt thou say if Christ be awake in thee, what manner of man am I, who wish to be avenged? Who am

I, who deal out threatenings against another man? I may die perhaps before I am avenged. And when at my last breath, inflamed with rage, and thirsting for vengeance, I shall depart out of this body, He will not receive me, Who did not wish to be avenged; He will not receive me, Who said, "Give, and it shall be given unto you; forgive, and it shall be forgiven you." Therefore will I refrain myself from my wrath, and return to the repose of my heart. Christ hath commanded the sea; tranquillity is restored.

Now what I have said as to anger, hold fast as a rule in all your temptations. A temptation has sprung up, it is the wind; thou art disturbed, it is a wave: awake up Christ then, let Him speak with thee. "Who is this, since the winds and the sea obey Him?" Who is this, Whom the sea obeyeth? "The sea is His, and He made it. All things were made by Him." Imitate the winds then, and the sea rather; obey the Creator. At Christ's command the sea giveth ear; and art thou deaf? The sea heareth, and the wind ceaseth, and dost thou still blow on? What! I say, I do, I devise; what is all this, but to be blowing on, and to be unwilling to stop in obedience to the Word of Christ? Let not the wave master you in this troubled state of your heart. Yet since we are but men, if the wind should drive us on, and stir up the affections of our souls, let us not despair; let us awake Christ that we may sail on a tranquil sea, and so come to our country.

Hom. on the New Testament. Hom. xiii.

Fourth Tuesday in Lent.

THE GOOD PHYSICIAN. S. AUGUSTINE.

THE Apostle Paul saith, "It is a faithful word and worthy of all acceptation, that Christ Jesus came into the world to save sinners, of whom I am first." None occasion was there for Christ the Lord's coming, but "to save sinners." Take away diseases, take away wounds, and there is no occasion for medicine. If a great Physician hath come from heaven, some great one was lying sick throughout the whole compass of the world. This sick one is the human race. "But all have not faith. The Lord knoweth them that are His." The Jews were proud, they lifted up themselves, they were high-minded, they thought themselves righteous, yea moreover, they belong to the "ninety and nine." What is "were left in the mountains?" Were left in earthly swelling. What is, "belong to the ninety and nine?" They are on the left hand, not on the right. For the ninety and nine are reckoned on the left hand; add one, you pass over to the right. He came then, as He Himself saith in another place; "The Son of Man came to seek and to save that which was lost." For the whole was lost; by the sin of one, in whom the whole was, the whole was lost. But One came without sin, to save from sin. But what is worst, by pride they were at once sick, and believed themselves to be sound.

They are the more dangerously sick, who through fevers have lost their mind. They laugh, and the sound weep. For a man in phrensy laughs, but he is not sound, yea moreover, he who is of sound mind weeps for the phrensied one who laughs. At first, if you propose these two things, which is best, to laugh or to weep? Who would not choose for himself to laugh? Yea, by reason of the wholesome sorrow of repentance, the Lord placed duty in weeping, blessings in laughing? How? When He said in the Gospel, "Blessed are they that weep, for they shall laugh." Duty then is in weeping, in laughing the reward of wisdom. For He puts laughing for joy, not its boisterous uproar, but exultation. If then you propose these two things, and ask which of them is best, to laugh, or to weep; every man would wish to laugh, and none to weep. Yet further, if you add certain persons to these affections, and propose it with the persons thus; "Which is best, to laugh in phrensy or to weep in sound mind?" a man would choose for himself weeping with soundness of mind, rather than laughter with madness. So great is the blessing of soundness of mind, that it is preferred even with weeping. These people who thought themselves sound, were much the more dangerously and desperately sick; and in this sickness whereby they had lost their minds, they even struck the Physician. Nay, not struck merely, but even killed Him. But He, even while He was being killed, was the Physician; He was beaten the while He was curing them; He endured the fury of the phrensied, yet did not desert the sick; He was seized, was bound, was struck with buffetings, received strokes with the reed, was derided, insulted, was brought to the judgment, condemned, hung upon the tree, they raged around him on every side, yet was He the Physician.

You recognised the phrensied people, recognise the Physician too. "Father, forgive them, for they know not what they do." They in madness were raging, and in their rage were shedding the Physician's blood; but He even of His very blood was making medicines for the sick. For in truth He did not say in vain, "Father, forgive them, for they know not what they do." The Christian prays, and his prayer is heard; Christ prayeth, and is not His prayer heard? For He who with the Father heareth prayer, in that He is God, how is He not heard as man, Which He was made for us? Undoubtedly He is heard. There they were, there they were raging; of them were those who blamed Him, and said, "Behold, He eateth with publicans and sinners." They were among that people, by whom the Physician Himself was being killed, and in His blood was being prepared an antidote even for them. For whereas the Lord not only poured out His blood, but expended even His death to prepare a medicine, He rose again to set forth an example of the resurrection. In His own patience He suffered, to teach our patience; and in His own resurrection He shewed for patience reward.

Hear the same Paul saying, "Awake thou that sleepest and arise from the dead, and Christ shall give thee light." Love not the bed of sin. "Thou hast turned (or made,) all his couch in his sickness," saith the Psalmist. Arise, be sound, love sound health, and go not through pride again from the right hand to the left, from the valley to the mountain, from lowliness to swelling. When thou shalt have been made whole, that is, when thou shalt have begun to live righteously, ascribe it to God, not to thine own self. For it was not by praising thyself that thou hast been made whole, but by pronouncing against thyself. For if through pride thou shalt praise thyself, thou wilt be more grievously sick. "For every one that exalteth himself shall be humbled, and he that humbleth himself shall be exalted."

Do not despair. Ye be sick, go unto Him and be healed; ye be blind, go unto Him and be enlightened. Both ye who are whole give Him thanks, and ye who are sick run to Him to be made whole; say all, "O come, let us adore, and fall down before Him; and weep before the Lord Who made us," both men and whole. For if He made us men, and we made ourselves whole; we have made something better than He. For a man whole, is better than a man merely. If then God made thee, and thou hast made thyself a good man, what thou hast made is the better. Lift not up thyself above God: submit thyself to God, adore, fall down before Him, confess to Him Who made thee; for no one recreateth, save He that createth; no one remaketh, save He Who made. This too in another Psalm, "He made us, and not we ourselves." Of a truth when He made thee thou hadst nothing to do; but when once thou art, thou hast thyself something to do; to run to the Physician, implore the Physician, Who is every where. And that thou mightest implore Him, He hath stirred up thy heart, and given thee the power to implore. "For it is God," saith He, "Who worketh in you both to will and to do of His good pleasure." For in order that thou mightest have a good will, His vocation preceded. Cry out, "My God, His mercy shall prevent me." That thou shouldest be, that thou shouldest feel, that thou shouldest listen, that thou shouldest consent, His mercy prevented thee. It hath prevented thee in all things; do thou too in some thing prevent His wrath. "In what?" you ask. Confess that in all these things whatever of good thou hast, thou hast from God; whatever of evil, from thyself. In thy good things despise not Him, nor praise thyself; and in thy evil things accuse not Him, nor excuse thyself; this is true confession. He Who hath in so many good things prevented thee, is to come to thee, and in examining His own gifts, and thy evil things, He maketh examination how thou shalt have used His good things. Therefore seeing that in all these gifts he hath prevented thee, do thou see wherein thou mayest prevent the face of Him Who is to come; hear the Psalm, "Let us prevent His face with confession. Let us prevent His Face:" before He come let Him be propitiated; before He is at hand let Him be appeased. For thou hast an High-Priest by Whom thou mayest appease thy God; yea, He is with the Father, Himself God to thee, Who is Man for thee. Accuse thyself, praise Him. By accusing thyself and praising Him Who made thee, He will come Who died for thee, and will quicken thee.

Lift ye up your hearts to be healed of sickness, and give thanks to God.

Sermons on the New Test. cxxv., cxxvi.

Fifth Wednesday in Lent.

PREVENTING GOD'S JUDGMENTS
S. CHRYSOSTOM.

IF thou desire not to be punished even here, pass judgment on thyself, exact thine own penalty. Listen to Paul, when he saith, "If we would judge ourselves, we should not be judged." If thou do this, proceeding in order, thou shalt even arrive at a crown.

But how are we to exact our own penalty? one may ask. Lament, groan bitterly, humble, afflict thyself, call to remembrance thy sins in their particulars. This thing is no small torture to a man's soul. If any man hath been in a state of contrition, he knows that the soul is punished by this more than any thing. If any hath been living in remembrance of sins, he knows the anguish thence arising. Therefore doth God appoint righteousness as a reward for such repentance, saying, "Declare thou, that thou mayest be justified." (Isa. xliii. 26.) Be then first to tell thy sin, that is. For it is not indeed a small step towards amendment, to lay together all our sins, and to be continually revolving and reckoning them up with their particulars. For he that is doing this will be so heart-broken as not to think himself worthy so much as to live; and he that thinks thus will be tenderer than any wax. For tell me not of great and notorious sins only, nor of things that are manifest, and acknowledged amongst all men; but lay together also thy secret crafts, and thy false accusations, and thine evil speakings, and thy vain-gloryings, and thine envy, and all such things. For neither will these bring a trifling punishment. For the reviler too shall fall into hell; and the drunkard hath no part in the kingdom; and he that loves not his neighbour so offends God as to find no help even in his own martyrdom, and he who overlooks the poor is sent into the fire.

Account not then these things to be little, but put all together, and write them as in a book. For if thou write them down, God blots them out; even as on the other hand, if thou omit writing them, God both inscribes them and exacts their penalty. It were then far better for them to be written by us, and blotted out above, than on the contrary, when we have forgotten them, for God to bring them before our eyes in that day.

Therefore that this may not be so, let us reckon up all with strictness, and we shall find ourselves answerable for much. For who is clear from covetousness? Nay, tell me not of the quantity, but since even in a small amount we shall pay the same penalty, consider this and repent. Who is rid of all insolence? Yet this casts into hell. Who hath not secretly spoken evil of his neighbour? Yet this deprives one of the kingdom. Who hath not been self-willed? Yet this man is more unclean than all. Who hath not looked with unchaste eyes? Yet this is a complete adulterer. Who hath not been angry with his brother without a cause? Yet such an one is in danger of the council. Who hath not sworn? Yet this thing is of the evil one. Who hath not forsworn himself? But this man is something more than of the evil one. Who hath not served Mammon? But this man is fallen away from the genuine service of Christ.

I have also other things greater than these to mention; but even these are enough, and able, if a man be not made to stone, nor utterly past feeling, to bring him to compunction. For if each one of them casts into hell, what will they not bring to pass when all are met together?

How then can any one be saved? it may be

asked. By application of the countervailing remedies; alms, prayers, compunction, repentance, humility, a contrite heart, contempt of possessions. For God hath marked out for us innumerable ways of salvation, if we be willing to attend.

Fasting brings no small power. For it both implants much strictness, and of a man makes an angel, and fights against the incorporeal powers; yet not by itself, but prayer too is needed, and prayer must come first. For what purpose did Christ go up into the mountain? To teach us that loneliness and retirement are good when we pray to God. With this view you see, He is continually withdrawing into the wilderness, and there often spends the whole night in prayer, teaching us earnestly to seek such quietness in our prayers, as the time and place may confer. For the wilderness is the mother of quiet; it is a calm and a harbour, delivering us from all turmoils. And blessings spring from both fasting and praying. For he that is praying as he ought, and fasting, hath not many wants, and he that hath not many wants cannot be covetous; he that is not covetous, will be also more disposed for almsgiving. He that fasts is light and winged, and prays with wakefulness, and quenches his wicked lusts, and propitiates God, and humbles his soul when lifted up. Therefore even the Apostles were almost always fasting. He that prays with fasting hath his wings double, and lighter than the very winds. And if thy body be too weak to fast continually, still it is not too weak for prayer.

Let us then give heed to these innumerable ways

of salvation, if we be willing to attend. Let us then attend, and let us every way cleanse out our wounds, shewing mercy, remitting our anger against them that have displeased us, giving thanks for all things to God, fasting according to our power, praying sincerely, "Making unto ourselves friends of the mammon of unrighteousness." For so shall we be able both to obtain pardon for our offences, and to win the promised good things; whereof may we all be counted worthy, by the grace and love towards man of our Lord Jesus Christ, to Whom be glory and might for ever and ever. Amen.

Homil. in S. Matt. xli., l., lvii.

Fifth Thursday in Lent.

CHRISTIAN ACTIVITY. S. CHRYSOSTOM.

"WORK out your own salvation with fear and trembling." How may this fear be produced? If we but consider that God is every where present, that He heareth all things, that He seeth all things, not only whatever is done and said, but also all that is in the heart, and in the depth of the soul; for He is "a discerner of the thoughts and intents of the heart;" if we so dispose ourselves, we shall not do or say or imagine aught that is evil. For tell me, if thou hadst to stand constantly near the person of a ruler, wouldest not thou stand there with fear? and how standing in God's Presence, dost thou not conceive fear and dread? Let it never be that thou despisest His long-suffering, for it is to bring thee to repentance that He is long-suffering; and when thou doest aught, never allow thyself to do it without being sensible that God is present in all things, for He *is* present. So then, whether eating or preparing to sleep, or giving way to passion, or robbing another, or whatever thou art about, consider that God is standing by, and thou wilt never be led into (overmuch) laughter, never be inflamed with rage. If this be thy thought continually, thou wilt continually be in "fear and trembling," forasmuch as thou art standing beside the King. The builder, though he be experienced, though he be perfectly master of his art, yet stands with fear and trembling, lest he fall down from the building. Thou too hast believed, thou hast performed many good deeds, thou hast mounted high; secure thyself, be in fear as thou standest, and keep a wary eye, lest thou fall thence. For manifold are the sorts of spiritual wickedness which aim to cast thee down. "Serve the Lord with fear," he says, "and rejoice unto Him with trembling." And how is *rejoicing* compatible with *trembling?* Yet this, be assured, is the only rejoicing; for when we perform some good work, and such as beseemeth those who do any thing with trembling, then only do we rejoice. "Work out your own salvation with fear and trembling;" he says not "*work*," but " work *out*," i. e. with much earnestness, with much diligence ; but as he had said, " with fear and trembling," and had thrown them into anxiety, see how he relieves their alarm ; for what does he say ? " It is God that worketh in you." Fear not because I said, "with fear and trembling ;" I said it not with this view, that thou shouldest give up in despair, that thou shouldest suppose virtue to be somewhat difficult to be attained, but that thou mightest be led to follow after it, and not spend thyself in vain pursuits; if this be the case, God will work all things. Do thou be bold ; "for it is God that worketh in you." If then He worketh, it is our part to bring a mind ever resolute, clenched, and unrelaxed. " For it is God that worketh in you both to will and to do." If He does Himself work in us to will, how dost thou exhort us ? for if He works Himself even the will, the words, which you speak to us, have no meaning. " That ye have obeyed," for we have not *obeyed:* it is without meaning that thou sayest, " with fear and trembling ;" for the whole is of God.

It was not for this that I said unto you, " for He worketh in you both to will and to do," but my object was to relieve your anxiety. If thou wilt, in that case He will "work in thee to will." Be not affrighted or wearied ; both the hearty desire and the accomplishment are a gift from Him: for where we have the will, thenceforward He will increase our will. For instance, I desire to do some good work ; He has wrought the good work itself, and by means of it He has wrought also the will. Or he says this in the excess of his piety, as when he declares that our well doings are gifts of grace.

As then when he calls these gifts, he does not put us out of the pale of free-will, but accords this to us; so when he says, "to work in us to will," he does not deprive us of free-will, but he shews that by actually doing right we greatly increase our heartiness in willing. For as doing comes of doing, so of not doing comes not doing. Hast thou given an alms? Thou art the more incited to give: but hast thou refused to give? thou art become so much the more disinclined. Hast thou practised temperance for one day? thou hast an incitement for the next likewise. Hast thou indulged to excess? thou hast increased the inclination to self-indulgence. "When the man cometh (into the depth of vice,) then cometh also contempt." (Prov. xviii. 3. Sept.) As then when a man descends into the depth of iniquity, he turns a despiser: so whosoever enters the depth of godliness, quickens his exertions. For as the one runs riot in despair, so the second, under a sense of the multitude of good things, exerts himself the more, fearing lest he should lose the whole. "According to his good pleasure," that is for love's sake, for the sake of pleasing Him; to the end that we may do that which is acceptable to Him; that the things may be done according to His Will. Here he shews and makes it a ground of confidence, that He is sure to work in us, for it is His Will that we live as He desires we should; and if He desires it, He Himself both worketh in us to this end, and will certainly accomplish it; for it is His Will that we live aright. Seest thou how S. Paul does not deprive us of free-will?

And further Paul added, "I count not myself to have apprehended," but I am solely engaged on "this one thing, in reaching forth unto the things which are before." For that is the meaning of "this one thing I do, forgetting those things which are behind, and reaching forth unto those things which are before, I press toward the mark for the prize of the high calling of God in Christ Jesus." Behold how, speaking thus, he shews what it was which made him reach forward unto the things which are before. He then who thinks that all is accomplished, and that nothing is wanting to him for the perfecting of virtue, may cease from running, as having apprehended all; but he who thinks that he is still distant from the goal, will never cease to run. This then we should always consider, even though we have wrought ten thousand good deeds; for if Paul after ten thousand deaths, after so many dangers, considered this, how much more should we? For I fainted not, saith he, although I availed not after running so much, nor did I despair, but I still run, I still strive. This thing only I consider, that I may in truth advance; thus too we should act; we should forget our successes, and throw them behind us, for the runner reckons not up how many circuits he hath finished, but how many are left. We too should reckon up, not how far we are advanced in virtue, but how much remains for us. For what doth that which is finished profit us, when that which is deficient is not added? Moreover, he did not say, do not reckon, nor remember, but, "forgetting," to make us more zealous, for we then become eager, when we apply all diligence to what is left, when we give to oblivion every thing else. "Reaching forth," saith he; before we arrive, we strive to obtain. For he reacheth forth who endeavours to outstrip his feet, though running with the rest of his body, stretching himself forward, and reaching out his hands, that he may accomplish somewhat more of the course. But this comes from great eagerness, from much warmth; thus the runner should run with great earnestness, with so great eagerness, without relaxation. As far as one who so runs differs from him who lies supine, so far doth Paul differ from us. He died daily, he was reproved daily, there was no season, there was no time in which his course advanced not. He wished not to take, but to snatch the prize; for in this way we may take it. He who giveth the prize standeth on high, the prize is laid up on high.

See how great a distance this is to run over! See how great is the ascent! Thither we must fly up with the wings of the Spirit, otherwise it is impossible to surmount this height. Thither must we go with the body, for it is allowed, "For our conversation is in Heaven," there is the prize. Seest thou the runners, how they live by rule, how they touch nothing that relaxes their strength, how they exercise themselves every day in the palæstra under a master and by rule? Do thou too imitate them, or rather exhibit greater eagerness, for the prizes are not equal. Many are those who would hinder you, live by rule: many are the things which relax your strength, make it agile for thy feet; for it is possible so to do, it comes not naturally, but by our will. Let us bring it to lightness, lest our swiftness of foot be hindered by the weight of other things. Teach thy feet to be sure, for there are many slippery places; and if thou fallest, straightway thou losest much. But yet if thou fall, rise up again. Even thus mayest thou obtain the victory. Never attempt slippery things, and thou wilt not fall; walk upon firm ground, up with thine head, up with thine eyes; these commands the trainers give to those who run. Thus thy strength is supported, but if thou stoopest downward thou fallest, thou art relaxed. Look upward, where the prize is; the sight of the prize increaseth the determination of our will; this hope suffereth not to perceive toil or distress, it maketh the distance appear short. And what is this prize? No palm-branch, but what? The kingdom of heaven, everlasting rest, glory together with Christ, the inheritance, brotherhood, ten thousand good things which it is impossible to name. It is impossible to describe the beauty of that prize; he who hath it alone knoweth it, and he who is about to receive it. It is not of gold, it is not of jewels, it is far more precious. Gold is mire in comparison with that prize, precious stones are mere bricks in comparison with its beauty. If thou hast this, and takest thy departure to heaven, thou wilt be able to walk there with great honour; the angels will reverence thee, when thou bearest this prize; with much confidence wilt thou approach them all, "in Christ Jesus." See the humility of the Apostle's mind, "this I do," saith he, "in Christ Jesus," for it is impossible without His assistance to pass over so vast an interval: we have need of much aid, of a mighty alliance; He hath willed that thou shouldst struggle below, on high He crowns thee. Not as in this world, the crown is not there where the contest is; but this crown is in that bright place. In Heaven thou receivest the prize.

In Philipp. Homil. viii. and xii.

Fifth Friday in Lent.

THE YOKE OF CHRIST. S. AUGUSTINE.

IT seems strange to some, brethren, when they hear the Lord say, "Come unto Me, all ye that labour and are heavy laden, and I will refresh you. Take My yoke upon you and learn of Me, for I am meek and lowly of heart, and ye shall find rest unto your souls. For My yoke is easy and My burden is light." And they consider that they who have carelessly bound their necks to this yoke, and have with much submission taken this burden upon their shoulders, are tossed about and exercised by so great difficulties in the world, that they seem not to be called from labour to rest, but from rest to labour rather ; since the Apostle also saith, " All who will live godly in Christ Jesus, shall suffer persecution." So one will say, How is the yoke easy, and the burden light, when to bear this yoke and this burden is nothing else but to live godly in Christ? And how is it said, " Come unto Me, all ye that labour and are heavy laden, and I will refresh you," and not rather said, " Come ye who are at ease and idle, that ye may labour?" For so He found those men idle and at ease, whom He hired into the vineyard, that they might bear the heat of the day.] And we hear the Apostle under that light yoke and easy burden say, " In all things approving ourselves as the Ministers of God, in much patience, in afflictions, in necessities, in distresses, in stripes," &c. And in another place of the same Epistle, " Of the Jews five times received I forty stripes save one. Thrice was I beaten with rods, once was I stoned, thrice have I suffered shipwreck, a night and a day have I been in the deep:" and the rest of the perils, which may be enumerated indeed, but endured they cannot be but by the help of the Holy Spirit.

All these grievous and heavy trials which he mentioned, did he very frequently and abundantly sustain; but in very deed the Holy Spirit was with him in the wasting of the outward man, to renew the inner man from day to day, and by the taste of spiritual rest in the affluence of the delights of God, to soften down by the hope of future blessedness all present hardships, and to alleviate all heavy trials. Lo, how sweet a yoke of Christ did he bear, and how light a burden! so that he could say that all those hard and grievous sufferings at the recital of which every hearer shudders, were a "light tribulation," as he beheld with the inward eyes, the eyes of faith, at how great a price of things temporal must be purchased the life to come, the escape from the everlasting pains of the ungodly, the full enjoyment, free from all anxiety, of the eternal happiness of the righteous. Men suffer themselves to be cut and burnt, that the pains not of eternity, but of some more lasting sore than usual may be bought off at the price of severer pain. For a languid and uncertain period, of a very short repose, and that too at the end of life, the soldier is worn down by all the hard trials of war, restless it may be for more years in his labours, than he will have to enjoy his rest in ease. To what storms and tempests, to what a fearful and tremendous raging of sky and sea, do the busy merchant-men expose themselves, that they may acquire riches inconstant as the wind, and full of perils and tempests, greater even than those by which they were acquired! What heats and colds, what perils from horses, from ditches, from precipices, from rivers, from wild beasts, do huntsmen undergo! what pain or hunger and thirst, what straitened allowances of the cheapest and meanest meat and drink, that they may catch a beast! and sometimes

THE YOKE OF CHRIST. 169

after all, the flesh of the beast for which they endure all this is of no use for the table.

Now in all these instances, they who do not love these things feel them as great severities; whereas they who love them endure the same, it is true, but they do not seem to feel them severe. For love makes all, the hardest and most distressing things, altogether easy, and almost nothing. How much more surely then and easily will charity do with a view to true blessedness, that which mere desire does as it can with a view to what is but misery! How easily is any temporal adversity endured, if it be that eternal punishment may be avoided, and eternal rest procured! Not without good reason did that vessel of election say with exceeding joy, "The sufferings of this present time are not worthy to be compared with the glory which shall be revealed in us." See then how it is that that "yoke is easy, and that burden light," and if it be strait to the few who choose it, yet it is easy to all who love it. The Psalmist saith, "Because of the words of Thy Lips I have kept hard ways," (Ps. xvi. 4. Sept.) But the things which are hard to those who labour, lose their roughness to those same men when they love. Wherefore it has been so arranged by the dispensation of the Divine Goodness, that to "the inner man who is renewed from day to day, placed no longer under the Law but under Grace, and freed from the burdens of numberless observances which were indeed a heavy yoke, but meetly imposed on a stubborn neck, every grievous trouble which that prince who is cast forth could inflict from without on the outward man, should through the easiness of a simple faith, and a good hope, and a holy charity, become light through the joy within. [For to a good will nothing is so easy as this good will to itself, and this is enough for God."] How much soever therefore this world may rage, most truly did the angels exclaim when the Lord was born in the flesh, "Glory to God in the highest, and on earth peace to men of good will;" because "His yoke," Who then was born, "is easy, and His burden light." And as the Apostle saith, "God is faithful, Who will not suffer us to be tempted above that we are able to bear; but will with the temptation also make a way to escape, that we may be able to bear it."

Serm. on the New Test., xx.

Fifth Saturday in Lent.

LONG-SUFFERING OF GOD. S. Chrys.

Dost thou find comfort in the delay of vengeance? Must we not of absolute necessity depart, and fall into the Hands of the Judge? What sort of comfort is it to be every day looking for punishment and vengeance? Nay if thou wouldest have some comfort from this delay, take it by gathering for thyself the fruit of amendment after repentance. Since if the mere delay of vengeance seem to thee a sort of refreshment, far more is it gain not to fall into the vengeance. Let us then make full use of this delay, in order to have a full deliverance from the dangers that press upon us. For none of the things enjoined is either burdensome or grievous, but all are so light and easy, that if we only bring a genuine purpose of heart, we may accomplish all, though we be chargeable with countless offences. For so Manasses had perpetrated innumerable pollutions, having both stretched out his hands against the saints, and brought abominations into the temple, and filled the city with murders, and wrought many other things beyond excuse; yet nevertheless after so long and so great wickedness, he washed away from himself all these things. How and in what manner? By repentance and consideration.

For there is not, yea there is not any sin that doth not yield and give way to the power of repentance, or rather to the grace of Christ. Since if we would but only change, we have Him to assist us. And if thou art desirous to become good, there is none to hinder us; or rather there is one to hinder us, the devil; yet hath he no power, so long as thou choosest what is best, and so attractest God to thine aid. But if thou art not thyself willing, but started aside, how shall He protect thee? Since not of necessity but of thine own will, He wills thee to be saved. For if thou thyself, having a servant full of hatred and aversion for thee, and continually going off and fleeing away from thee, wouldest not choose to keep him, and this though needing his services; much less will God, who doeth all things not for His own profit but for thy salvation, choose to retain thee by compulsion; as on the other hand, if thou shew forth a right intention only, He would not choose ever to give thee up, no, not whatever the devil may do. So that we are to blame for our own destruction. Because we do not approach, nor beseech, nor intreat Him, as we ought; but even if we do draw nigh, it is not as persons who have need to receive, neither is it with the proper faith, nor as making demand, but we do all in a gaping and listless way.

And yet God would have us demand things of Him, and for this accounts Himself greatly bound to thee. For He alone of all debtors, when the demand is made, counts it a favour, and gives what we have not lent Him. And if He should see him pressing earnestly that makes the demand, He pays down even what He hath not received of us; but if sluggishly, He too keeps on making delays; not through unwillingness to give, but because He is pleased to have the demand made upon Him by us. For this cause He told thee also the example of that friend, who came by night, and asked a loaf, (S. Luke xi. 5—8,) and of the judge that feared not God, nor regarded men. (S. Luke xviii. 1—8.) And He stayed not at similitudes, but signified it also in His very actions, when He dismissed that Phœnician woman, having filled her with His great gift. For through her He signified, that He gives to them that ask earnestly, even the things that pertain not to them. "For it is not meet," saith He, "to take the children's bread, and give it unto the dogs." But for all that He gave, because she demanded of Him earnestly. But by the Jews He shewed, that to them that are careless, He gives not even their own. They accordingly received nothing, but lost what was their own. And while these, because they asked not, did not receive so much as their very own, she, because she assailed Him with earnestness, had power to obtain even what pertained to others, and the dog received what was the children's. So great a good is importunity. For though thou be a dog, yet being importunate, thou shalt be preferred to the child being negligent; for what things affection accomplishes not, these, all of them importunity did accomplish. Say not therefore, "God is an enemy to me, and will not hearken." He doth straightway answer thee, continually troubling Him, if not because thou art His friend, yet because of thine importunity. And neither the enmity, nor the unseasonable time, nor any thing else, becomes an hinderance. Say not, "I am unworthy, and do not pray;" for such was the Syrophœnician woman too. Say not, "I have sinned much, and am not able to intreat Him Whom I have angered," for God looks not at the desert, but at the disposition. For if the ruler that feared not God, neither was ashamed of men, was overcome by the widow, much more will He that is good be won over by continual intreaty.

So that though thou be no friend, though thou be

not demanding thy due, though thou hast devoured thy Father's substance, and have been a long time out of sight; though without honour, though last of all, though thou approach Him angry, though much displeased; be willing only to pray and to return, and thou shalt receive all, and shalt quickly extinguish the wrath and condemnation.

But behold I pray, saith one, and there is no result. Why thou prayest not like those; such I mean as the Syrophœnician woman, the friend that came late at night, and the widow that is continually troubling the judge, and the son that consumed his father's goods. For didst thou so pray thou wouldest quickly obtain. For though despite have been done unto Him, yet is He a Father; and though He have been provoked to anger, yet is He fond of His children; and one thing only doth He seek, not to take vengeance for our affronts, but to see thee repenting and intreating Him. Would that we were warned in like measure, as those bowels are moved to love for us. But this fire seeks a beginning only, and if thou afford it a little spark, thou kindlest a full flame of beneficence. For not because He hath been insulted is He sore vexed, but because it is thou who art insulting Him, and so becoming frenzied. For if we being evil, when our children molest us, grieve on their account, much more is God, Who cannot so much as suffer insult, sore vexed on account of thee, who hast committed it. If we, who love by nature, much more He, Who is kindly affectioned beyond nature, "For though," saith He, "a woman should forget the fruit of her womb, yet will I not forget thee."

Let us therefore draw nigh unto Him, and say, "Truth, Lord; for even the dogs eat of the crumbs which fall from their master's table." Let us draw nigh "in season, out of season:" or rather, one can never draw nigh out of season, for it is unseasonable not to be continually approaching. For of Him Who desires to give it is always seasonable to ask; yea, as breathing is never out of season, so neither is praying unseasonable, but rather not praying. Since as we need this breath, so also do we the help that comes from Him; and if we be willing, we shall easily draw Him to us. And the Prophet, to manifest this, and to point out the constant readiness of His beneficence, said, "We shall find Him prepared as the morning." (Hosea vi. 3. Sept.) For as often as we may draw nigh, we shall see Him awaiting our movements. And if we fail to draw from out of His ever-springing goodness, the blame is all ours. This, for example, was His complaint against certain Jews, when He said, "My mercy is as a morning cloud, and as the early dew it goeth away." And His meaning is like this, "I indeed have supplied all My part, but ye, as a hot sun coming over scatters both the cloud and the dew, and makes them vanish, so have ye by your great wickedness restrained the unspeakable beneficence."

Which also itself again is an instance of providential care; that even when He sees us unworthy to receive good, He withholds His benefits, lest He render us careless. But if we change a little, even but so much as to know that we have sinned, He gushes out beyond the fountains, He is poured forth beyond the ocean; and the more thou receivest so much the more doth He rejoice; and in this way is stirred up again to give us more. For indeed He accounts it as His own wealth, that we should be saved, and that He should give largely to them that ask. And this, it may seem, Paul was declaring when he said that He is "rich unto all, and over all that call upon Him." Because when we pray not, then He is wroth; when we pray not, then doth He turn away from us. For this cause "He became poor, that He might make us rich;" for this cause He underwent all those sufferings, that He might incite us to ask.

Let us not therefore despair, but having so many motives and good hopes, though we sin every day, let us approach Him, intreating, beseeching, asking the forgiveness of our sins. For thus we shall be more backward to sin for the time to come; thus shall we drive away the devil, and shall call forth the loving-kindness of God, and attain unto the good things to come, by the grace and love towards man of our Lord Jesus Christ, to Whom be glory and might for ever and ever. Amen.

Homil. in S. Matt. xxii.

Passion Sunday.

THANKFULNESS. S. CHRYSOSTOM.

BEARING these things in mind, let us also fulfil all our duties to our neighbours, and to God let us give thanks continually. For it is too monstrous, enjoying as we do His bounty in deed every day, not so much as in word to acknowledge the favour; and this though the acknowledgement again yield all its profit to us. Since He needs not, be sure, any thing of ours; but we stand in need of all things from Him. Thus thanksgiving itself adds nothing to Him, but causes us to be nearer to Him. For if men's bounties, when we call them to memory, do the more warm us with their proper love-charm, much more when we are continually bringing to mind the whole acts of our Lord towards us, shall we be more diligent in regard of His commandments.

For this cause also Paul said, "Be ye thankful." For the best preservative of any benefit is the remembrance of the benefit, and a continual thanksgiving.

For this cause even the awful mysteries, so full of that great salvation, which are celebrated at every Communion, are called a Sacrifice of thanksgiving; because they are the commemoration of many benefits, and they signify the very sum of God's care for us, and by all means they work upon us to be thankful. For if His being born of a pure Virgin was a great miracle, and the Evangelist said in amaze, "Now all this was done;" His being also slain; what place shall we find for that? tell me, I mean, if to be born is called so much; to be crucified, and to pour forth His Blood, and to give Himself to us for a spiritual Feast and Banquet; what can that be called? Let us therefore give Him thanks continually, and let this precede both our words and our works.

But let us be thankful not for our own blessings alone, but also for those of others; for in this way we shall be able both to destroy our envy, and to rivet our charity, and make it more genuine. Since it will not even be possible for thee to go on envying those, in behalf of whom thou givest thanks to the Lord.

Wherefore, as you know, the priest also enjoins to give thanks for the world, for the former things, for the things that are now, for what hath been done to us before, for what shall befall us hereafter, when that Sacrifice is set forth. For this is the thing both to free us from earth, and to receive us into heaven, and to make us angels instead of men. Because they too form a choir, and give thanks to God for His good things bestowed on us, saying, "Glory to God in the highest, and on earth peace; good will towards men." Do ye ask, what is this to us that are not upon earth, nor are men? Nay, it is very much to us, for we have been taught so to love our fellow servants, as even to account their blessings ours. Wherefore Paul also, every where in his Epistles, gives thanks for God's gracious acts to the world.

Let us too therefore continually give thanks, for our own blessings, and for those of others; alike for the small and for the great. For though the gift be small, it is made great by being God's gift; or rather, there is nothing small that cometh from Him, not only because it is bestowed by Him, but also in its very nature.

And to pass over all the rest, which exceed the sand in multitude, what is equal to the dispensation that hath taken place for our sake? In that, what was more precious to Him than all, even His Only-begotten Son, Him He gave for us His enemies; and not only gave, but after giving, did even set Him before us as Food: Himself doing all things that were for our good, both in giving Him, and in making us thankful for all this. For because man is for the most part unthankful, He doth Himself every where take in hand and bring about what is for our good. And what He did with respect to the Jews, by places and times and feasts, reminding them of His benefits; that He did in this case also, by the manner of the Sacrifice, bringing us to a perpetual remembrance of His bounty in these things.

No one hath so laboured that we should be approved, and great and in all things right-minded, as the God Who made us. Wherefore both against our will He befriends us often, and without our knowledge oftener than not. And if thou marvel at what I have said, I point to this as having occurred not to any ordinary person, but to the blessed Paul. For even that blessed man, when in much danger and affliction, often besought God, that the temptations might depart from him; nevertheless God regarded not his request, but his profit, and to signify this He said, "My grace is sufficient for thee, for My strength is made perfect in weakness." So that before He hath told him the reason, He benefits him against his will, and without his knowing it.

Now what great thing doth He ask, in requiring us to be thankful in return for such tender care? Let us then obey, and every where keep this. Since neither were the Jews by any thing ruined so much as by being unthankful; those many stripes, one after another, were brought upon them by nothing else than this; or rather, even before those stripes this had ruined and corrupted their soul. "For the hope of the unthankful," saith one, "is like the winter's hoar frost," (Wisdom xvi. 29,) it benumbs and deadens the soul, as that doth our bodies.

And this springs from pride, and from thinking one's-self worthy of something. But the contrite will acknowledge grounds of thanksgiving to God, not for good things only, but also for what seem to be adverse; and how much soever he may suffer, will count none of his sufferings undeserved. Let us then also, the more we advance in virtue, so much the more make ourselves contrite; for indeed this, more than any thing else, is virtue. Because as the sharper our sight is, the more thoroughly do we learn how distant we are from the sky; so the more we advance in virtue, so much the more are we instructed in the difference between God and us. And this is no small part of true wisdom, to be able to perceive our own desert. For he best knows himself, who accounts himself to be nothing. Thus we see that both David and Abraham when they were come up to the highest pitch of virtue, then best fulfilled this; and would call themselves the one, "earth and ashes," (Gen. xviii. 27;) the other, "a worm," (Ps. ii. 7;) and all the saints too, like these, acknowledge their own wretchedness. So that he surely who is lifted up in boasting, is the very person to be most ignorant of himself. Wherefore also in our common practice we are wont to say of the proud, "he knows not himself," "he is ignorant of himself." And he that knows not himself, whom will he know? For as he that knows himself will know all things, so he who knows not this, neither will he know the rest.

Such an one was he that saith, "I will exalt my throne above the heavens," (Isa. xiv. 13. Sept.) Being ignorant of himself, he was ignorant of all else. But not so Paul; he rather used to call himself "one born out of due time," and last of the saints, and did not account himself to be worthy so much as of the title of the Apostles, after so many and so great deeds of goodness.

Him therefore let us emulate and follow. And

we shall follow him, if we rid ourselves of earth, and of things on earth. For nothing makes a man to be so ignorant of himself, as the being rivetted to worldly concerns; nor does any thing again so much cause men to be rivetted to worldly concerns, as ignorance of one's-self; for these things depend upon each other. I mean, that as he that is fond of outward glory, and highly esteems the things present, if he strive for ever is not permitted to understand himself; so he that overlooks these things will easily know himself; and having come to the knowledge of himself, he will proceed in order to all the other parts of virtue.

In order therefore that we may learn this good knowledge, let us, disengaged from all the perishable things that kindle in us so great flame, and made aware of their vileness, show forth all lowliness of mind, and self-restraint; that we may attain unto blessings both present and future, by the grace and love towards man of our Lord Jesus Christ, with Whom, &c.

Homil. in S. Matt. xxv.

Monday in Passion Week.

DANGER OF SELF-INDULGENCE. S. Chrys.

Nothing is so unbecoming in a Christian, and foreign to his character, as to seek ease and rest. Nothing is so foreign to our profession and enlistment, as to be engrossed with the present life. Thy Master was Crucified, and dost thou seek ease? Thy Master was pierced with nails, and dost thou live delicately? Do these things become a noble soldier? Wherefore Paul saith, "Many walk of whom I have told you often, and now tell you even weeping, that they are enemies to the Cross of Christ." Since there were some who made a pretence of Christianity, yet lived in ease and luxury. This is contrary to the Cross: wherefore he thus spoke. For the Cross belongs to a soul to die at its post for the fight, longing to die, seeking nothing like ease; whilst their conversation is of the contrary sort. So that if they say they are of Christ, still they are enemies of the Cross. For did they love the Cross, they would strive to live a life befitting the Cross. Was not thy Master hung upon the tree? Imitate Him in some other way, if thou canst not in His own. Crucify thyself, though no one crucify thee. Crucify thyself I say, not that thou mayest slay thyself, God forbid, for that is a wicked thing; but as Paul said, "The world is crucified to me, and I unto the world." If thou lovest thy Master, die His death. Learn how great is the power of the Cross; how many goods it hath attained, and doth still; how it is the safety of our life. Through it all things are done. Baptism is through the Cross, for we must receive that seal: the laying on of hands is through the Cross. If we are in the way, if we are at home, wherever we are, the Cross is a great good, the armour of salvation, a shield which cannot be beaten down, a weapon to oppose the devil; thou bearest the Cross when thou art at enmity with him, not simply when thou sealest thyself by it, but when thou sufferest the things belonging to the Cross. Christ thought fit to call our sufferings by the name of the Cross: as when He saith, "Except a man take up his cross and follow Me," i. e. except he be prepared to die. But these being vile, and lovers of life, and lovers of their bodies, are enemies of the Cross. And every one who is a friend of luxury and present safety, is an enemy of that Cross in which Paul makes his boast, which he embraces, with which he desires to be incorporated; as when he saith, " I am crucified unto the world, and the world unto me." But here he saith, "I now tell you weeping." Wherefore? Because the evil was urgent, because such deserve tears. Of a truth the luxurious are worthy of tears, who make fat that which is thrown about them, I mean the body, and take no thought of that soul which must give account. Behold thou livest delicately, behold thou art drunken, to-day and to-morrow, ten years, twenty, thirty, fifty, a hundred, (which is impossible, but if thou wilt, let us suppose it.) What is the end? What is the gain? Nought at all. Doth it not then deserve tears and lamentations, to lead such a life? God hath brought us into this course that He may crown us, and we take our departure without doing any noble action? Wherefore Paul weepeth, when others laugh and live in pleasure. So feeling is he; such thought taketh he for all men. "Whose god," saith he, "is their belly." For this have they a god! that is, "Let us eat and drink." Dost thou see how great an evil luxury is? to some their wealth, and to others their belly is their god. Are not these too idolators, and worse than the common? "Whose glory," saith he, "is in their shame." It is a fearful thing to do shameful actions, but to do them and be ashamed, is only half so dreadful. But where a man even boasts himself of them, it is excessive senselessness.

Do these words apply to them (to whom S. Paul wrote) alone? and do those who are here present escape the charge? Will no one have account to render of these things? Does no one make a god of his belly, or glory in his shame? When one consumes his whole life in revelling, and expends some small trifle on the poor, whilst he consumes the larger portion on his belly, will not these words with justice apply to him? No words are more apt to call attention, or more cutting in reproof than these, "Whose god is their belly, whose glory is in their shame." And who are these? They who mind earthly things; who say, Let us build houses. Where, I ask? On the earth, they answer. Let us purchase farms; on the earth again: let us obtain powers; again on the earth: let us enrich ourselves; all these things are on the earth. These are they whose god is their belly, for if they have no spiritual thoughts, but have all their possessions here, and mind these things, with reason have they their belly for their god, in saying, " Let us eat and drink, for to-morrow we die." And then thou grievest about thy body, that it is of earth, though this doth thee no injury in respect of virtue. But whilst thou draggest thy soul to the earth with luxury, and takest no heed of this, tell me, dost thou laugh, and art overjoyed? And what pardon wilt thou obtain for thy utter want of feeling? when thou oughtest to render even thy body spiritual, for thou mayest if thou wilt. Thou hast received a belly that thou mayest feed, not distend it; that thou mayest have the mastery over it, not have it as mistress over thee: that it may minister to thee for the nourishment of the other parts, not that thou mayest minister to it, not that thou mayest exceed limits. The sea when it passes its bounds, doth not work so many evils as the belly doth to our body, together with our soul. The former overfloweth all the earth, the latter all the body. Put moderation for a boundary to it, as God hath put the sand for the sea: then if its waves arise and rage furiously, rebuke it with the power which is in thee. See how God hath honoured thee with reason, that thou mightest imitate

Him, and thou wilt not; but when thou seest it overflowing, destroying, and overwhelming thy whole nature, darest not to restrain and moderate it.

"Whose god," he saith, "is their belly." Let us see how Paul served God: let us see how gluttons serve their belly. Do not they undergo innumerable deaths? do not they fear to disobey whatever it orders? do not they minister impossibilities to it? Are they not worse than slaves? But Paul was not such. Wherefore he said, "Our conversation is in heaven." Let us not then seek for ease here, let us wish to shine there, where our conversation is, "from whence also," saith he, "we look for the Saviour, the Lord Jesus Christ, Who shall change our vile body, that it may be fashioned like unto His glorious Body." By little and little hath he carried us up. He saith, "from heaven," and "our Saviour," shewing from the place, and from the Person, the dignity of the subject. "Who shall change our vile body," saith he. Our body now suffereth many things; it is bound with chains, it is scourged, it suffereth innumerable things; but the Body of Christ suffered the same.

He saith "our vile body," because it is now humbled, subject to destruction, to pain, because it seemeth to be worthless, and to have nothing beyond that of other animals. "That it may be fashioned like unto His glorious Body." What! shall this our body be fashioned like unto Him, Who sitteth at the Right Hand of the Father, to Him Who is worshipped by the angels, before Whom do stand the incorporeal powers, to Him Who is above all rule and power and might? If then the whole world were to take up weeping and lament for those who have fallen from this hope, could it worthily lament? because when a promise is given us of our body being made like unto Him, it still departs with the devils. I speak not of hell now; whatever can be said, I consider nothing to this falling off. What sayest thou, O Paul? to be made like unto Him? Yes, he answered; then lest you should disbelieve he addeth a reason; "according to the working whereby He is able even to subdue all things unto Himself." He hath power to subdue all things unto Himself, wherefore also destruction and death. Or rather, He doth this with the same power. For tell me, which requireth the greater power, to subject demons and Angels and Archangels, and Cherubim and Seraphim, or to make the body incorruptible and immortal? The latter certainly (would He do) rather than the former; He shewed forth the greater works of His power, that you might believe these too. Wherefore though ye see these men rejoicing and honoured, yet stand firm; be not offended at them, be not moved. These our hopes are sufficient to raise up even the most sluggish and indolent. All we have, saith he, is in the heavens. Our Saviour, our city, whatever a man can name: "whence we look for the Saviour, the Lord Jesus Christ." And this is an act of His kindness and love towards man. He Himself again cometh to us. He doth not drag us thither, but takes us, and so departs with us. And this is a mark of great honour; for if He came to us when we were enemies, much rather doth He even when we are become friends. He doth not commit this to angels, nor to servants, but Himself cometh in the clouds, to call us to His royal mansion. And perchance His own as honoured by Him, shall be carried through the clouds; for we, saith he, who honour Him, " shall be caught up in the clouds, and so shall we be ever with the Lord."

Who then is found " a faithful and wise servant?" Who are they that are deemed worthy of such good things? How miserable are those that fail! For if, after losing the kingdom we were for ever to weep, should we do all we ought? For were you to make mention of hells innumerable, you would name nothing equal to that pain which the soul then sustaineth, when all the world is in confusion, when the trumpets are sounding, when the angels are rushing forward, the ten thousand ranks are pouring forth upon the earth, the Cherubim and Seraphim; when He Himself is coming, with His ineffable glory; when those meet Him, who had gone to gather the elect into the midst; when Paul, and all who in his time had been approved are crowned, are proclaimed aloud, are honoured by the King, before all His heavenly host. Hell I confess is intolerable, yea, very intolerable, but more intolerable than it is the loss of the kingdom.

Consider of how great glory we shall be deprived, when it is in our power not to be deprived of it. For this is the misery, that we suffer these things, when it is in our power not to suffer them. For when Christ receiveth the one part to His Father in heaven, and rejecteth the other, whom angels take and drag against their will, weeping and hanging down their heads, to the fire of hell when they have first been made a spectacle to the whole world, what grief, think you, is there? Let us then make haste, while there is time, and take great thought of our own salvation. How many things have we to say, like the rich man? If any one would now suffer us, we would take counsel of the things that are profitable! But no one doth suffer us. And that we shall say so is clear, not from him alone, but from many others. And that you may learn this, how many men have been in fevers, and said, If we should recover we would not again fall into the same state. Many such words we shall then say, but we shall be answered as the rich man was, that there is a gulf, that we have received our good things here. Let us groan then I intreat you, bitterly; rather let us not only groan, but pursue virtue too; let us lament now for salvation, that we may not then lament in vain. Let us weep now, and we shall not weep then at our evil lot. This weeping is of virtue; that of unprofitable reflection: let us afflict ourselves now, that we may not then; for it is not the same thing to be afflicted here and there. For here thou art afflicted for a little time, rather thou dost not perceive thy affliction, knowing that thou art afflicted for thy good. But there the affliction is more bitter, because it is not in hope, nor for any escape, but without limit, and throughout.

But we may all be freed from this, and obtain forgiveness. But since there is need of intense diligence and ceaseless prayer, that we may not fail of this, let us, I beg, be diligent; if we are diligent, we prevail through our prayer: if we pray earnestly, God grants our request; but if we ask Him not, nor do earnestly aught of this sort, nor work, how is it possible that we who sleep should ever succeed? By no means. For it is much if even by running, and exerting ourselves, and being conformed to His death, as Paul said, we shall be able to succeed, not to say sleeping. "If by any means I may attain," saith he. But if Paul said, "if by any means I may attain," what shall we say? For it is not possible that they who slumber should accomplish even worldly business, not to say spiritual. They who slumber cannot receive aught from their friends, far less from God. Let us labour for a little time, that we may have rest for ever. We must at all events be afflicted. If we are not afflicted here, it awaits us there. Why choose we not to be afflicted here, that there we may have rest? May we all, having had our conversation worthy of Christ, and having been conformed to His death, obtain the unspeakable joys in Christ Jesus with Whom, &c.

In Philip. Homil. xiii.

Tuesday in Passion Week.

PATIENCE. S. CYPRIAN.

PATIENCE begins from God, from Him its brightness and dignity takes its source. The origin and greatness of patience proceeds from God its Author. Man ought to love that thing which is dear to God. The Divine Majesty in loving that which is good, commends it. If God is our Lord and Father, let us follow after the patience of Him Who is both Lord to us and Father, for it belongs to servants to be obedient, and it becomes not children to be degenerate. But in God what patience and how abundant is it, that in the contempt of His Majesty and honour, most patiently enduring profane temples instituted by men, and earthen images, and sacrilegious rites, He makes the day to spring and the light of the sun to arise, equally on the evil and the good! And when He waters the earth with rain, none is excluded from His bounties, but alike on the just and the unjust He yields the undistinguished showers. We see, according to an impartial equality of patience, for sinful men and for innocent; for the religious and the impious; for them that thank Him and for the unthankful, at the nod of God seasons obeying them, elements serving them, winds breathing, fountains flowing, the crops of corn swelling, fruits of the vineyard mellowing, trees stocked with apples, groves putting on their verdure, and meadows flowering. And while God is offended by frequent, yea, by unceasing sins, He refrains His wrath, and patiently awaits for the day of retribution once for all appointed. And while He has vengeance in His power, He rather long keeps patience; enduring that is in His compassion, and putting off, to the end that if it be possible a wickedness long continuing may one time change, and men involved in the contagion of errors and sins, though late, may yet turn to the Lord, according to His Own warning and instruction; "I have no pleasure in the death of him that dieth, but rather that he should return and live." And again the Prophet, "Return to the Lord your God, for He is gracious and merciful and patient, and of great pity, and repenteth Him toward the evil which He hath inflicted." This also the blessed Apostle Paul repeating and calling back the sinner to repentance, sets forth and says, "Or despisest thou the riches of His goodness, and forbearance and long-suffering, not knowing that the patience and goodness of God leadeth thee to repentance? But after thy hardness and impenitent heart thou treasurest up unto thyself wrath in the day of wrath, and of revelation of the righteous judgment of God, Who will render to every man according to his deeds." He calls God's judgment just, because it is late, because it is long and much postponed; that by the long patience of God man may gain provision unto life. And penalty is then revealed upon the ungodly and the sinner, when patience can now no more avail the offender.

And that we may be enabled, dearest brethren, more fully to understand that patience is a thing of God, and that whoever is kind and patient and mild, is an imitator of God his Father, therefore was it that the Lord giving in His Gospel instructions unto salvation, and drawing forth divine admonitions in order to form His disciples unto perfection, set it forth and said, "Ye have heard that it is said, Thou shalt love thy neighbour, and hate thine enemy; but I say unto you, Love your enemies, and pray for them which persecute you, that ye may be the children of your Father Which is in heaven, Who maketh His sun to rise on the good and on the evil, and raineth on the just and on the unjust. For if ye love them which love you, what reward shall ye have; do not even the publicans the same? Be ye therefore perfect, even as your Father Which is in heaven is perfect." He saith that thus we become perfect sons of God; thus He shewed and taught we are brought unto fulness, after being made again in heavenly birth, if the patience of God our Father abide in us, if the divine likeness which Adam had lost by sin, become manifested and shine forth in our acts.

Neither, dearest brethren, did Jesus Christ our God and Lord only teach us this in words, but fulfilled it also in His deeds. And since He had said that to this end He came down to do the Will of His Father, among the other wonders of His virtues, by which He expressed the proofs of a divine

Majesty, He preserved also the patience of His Father, by continuance of endurance. In fine, all actions, even from His first coming, are marked out by patience as their companion; because first descending out of that heavenly height, into earthly places, the Son of God scorned not to put on the flesh of man; and while He Himself was not a sinner, to bear the sins of others. Meantime putting off His immortality, He suffers Himself to be made mortal, that He, the Innocent, may be slain for the salvation of the guilty. The Lord is baptized by the servant, and He Who was to give remission of sins, Himself disdains not to wash His Body in the "laver of regeneration." He for forty days doth fast by Whom all others are fattened; He hungers and suffers famine that they who had been in famine of the Word and of grace, may be filled with bread of heaven. He withstands the devil tempting Him, and content with only having conquered His foe, contends against him no longer than by words. He did not preside over His disciples as over servants in a Lord's power, but gently and mildly He loved them with a brother's affection. He condescended also to wash the feet of the Apostles, that since He, being Lord, dealt thus toward His servants, He might by His example teach what manner of man a fellow-servant ought to be towards his fellows and equals. Nor need it be wondered at, that He became such unto the obedient, Who in long patience could bear with Judas even unto extremity, taking food with His enemy, knowing the domestic foe, yet not publicly revealing him, nor refusing the kiss of the betrayer. Moreover, in His bearing with the Jews, how great was His equanimity, and how great His patience! Bending the unbelieving unto faith by persuading them, softening the unthankful by yielding to them, answering with gentleness to them that used contradiction, in clemency bearing with the proud, and with humility giving way to the persecutors; even unto the hour of His Cross and Passion ready to gather together men who slew the prophets, and were ever rebellious against God. And in His very Passion and Cross, before they were come to the cruelty of death and the shedding of blood, what reproaches of reviling were patiently heard by Him, what sufferings of contumely endured, so that He received with patience the spittings of revilers, Who a little before had with His spittle made eyes for a blind man; and He in Whose Name the devil with his angels is now by His servants scourged, Himself suffered scourging; He was crowned with thorns Who crowns martyrs with eternal flowers; He smitten on the Face with palms Who yields true palms to them that conquer; He stripped of His earthly raiment Who clothes others with the robe of immortality; He received gall for food Who gave the food of heaven; and He had vinegar to drink Who instituted the Cup of Salvation. He innocent, He just; yea Innocency itself and Justice itself, is numbered with the transgressors; and Truth is pressed with false testimonies, the future Judge is judged, and the Word of God led in silence to the slaughter. And while the stars are confounded before the Cross of the Lord, the elements disturbed, earth quakes, night shuts out the day; and the sun, so he be not forced to witness the crime of the Jews, draws back both his rays and his eyes. He speaks not and moves not, nay in His very Passion makes no profession of His Majesty: all things even unto the end are perseveringly and unceasingly endured, to the end that a full and perfect patience may be finished in Christ. And after all these things He gives acceptance even to His murderers, if they come turning unto Him; and with saving patience, bountiful to preserve, He shuts His Church to none; those adversaries, those blasphemers, those ever enemies of His Name, if they do penitence for their sin, if they acknowledge the crime they had committed, He admits not only to forgiveness of their wickedness, but even to the reward of a heavenly kingdom. What can be named more patient, or more bounteous? The man is quickened by the Blood of Christ, men who shed Christ's Blood. Such and so great is the patience of Christ; had it not been such and so great, neither had the Church had Paul for an Apostle. But if we also, dearest brethren, are in Christ, if we put Him on, if He is the Way of our salvation, let us, following Christ's steps in the paths of salvation, walk in the example of Christ, as John the Apostle instructs us, saying, "he who saith he abideth in Christ ought himself also so to walk as He walked." Peter likewise, on whom the Church was founded by the good pleasure of the Lord, lays it down in his Epistle, and says, "Christ suffered for us, leaving you an example, that ye should follow His steps; Who did not sin, neither was deceit found in His Mouth; Who when He was reviled, reviled not again; when He suffered He threatened not, but delivered Himself to him that unjustly judged Him."

In fine, we find both patriarchs and prophets and all the just who in an antecedent image bare the figure of Christ, did nothing rather guard in the praise of their virtues, than the keeping hold of patience in firm and fixed evenness of mind. Thus Abel, first to initiate and consecrate martyrdom in its origin and the passion of a just man, resists not, strives not against the fratricide; but is killed, humble and meek through patience. Thus Abraham believing God and first laying the root and foundation of faith, tempted in his son, hesitates not nor delays, but obeys the command of God with an entire patience of devotion. And Isaac made before in figure after the likeness of the Lord's Sacrifice, when brought to be immolated of his father, is found patient; and Jacob driven forth by his brother, departs out of his country patiently; and with greater patience afterwards, he as a suppliant draws him back to concord, when yet more impious and persecuting by peaceable presents. Joseph, sold and banished by his brethren, not only patiently pardons them, but also largely and mercifully distributes free gifts of corn to them at their coming to him. Moses is oftentimes despised by an unthankful and unfaithful people, and is almost stoned by them, and yet mildly and patiently he entreated the Lord for that people. But in David, of whom according to the flesh Christ's Nativity sprang, how great and wonderful and Christian a patience, to have had it within his hand to be able oftentimes to slay King Saul when persecuting and desiring to kill him; and yet to love rather to save him when placed in his power and delivered over to him, not rendering back a return to his enemy, nay beyond this, avenging him when he was killed! So many prophets in fine were slain; so many martyrs honoured with glorious deaths, who all came to heavenly crowns by the praise of patience. For neither can the crown of pains and patience be obtained, except in that pain and passion, patience go before. But that it may be more manifestly and more fully known, dearest brethren, how useful and necessary is patience, let the sentence of God be meditated on, which Adam, unmindful of the commandment and transgression of the law which had been given him, received in the first beginning of the world, and of the human race; thence we learn how patient we ought to be in this life, who are in such state born, as to labour here with distresses and conflicts. "Because," He saith, "thou hast hearkened unto the voice of thy wife, and hast eaten of the tree, of which alone I had commanded thee that thou shouldest not eat, cursed shall be the ground in all thy works; in sorrow and in groaning shalt thou eat of it all the days of thy life; thorns and thistles shall it yield to thee, and thou shalt eat the herb of the field; in the sweat of thy face thou shalt eat thy bread, till thou return unto the ground from which thou wast taken; for dust thou art, and unto dust shalt thou return."

By the bond of this sentence we all are tied and fastened, until death being done away we depart out of this life. In sorrow and groaning it is needful that we be, all the days of our life; it is needful we eat bread with sweat and toil; wherefore each one of us when he is born and is received in the hostelry of this world, makes his start in tears; and although ignorant and unaware of all things, in that very beginning of birth he has learnt no other thing than weeping. By a providence of nature he moans the anxieties of mortal life, and the unfashioned soul does in its very entrance by wailing and groaning testify to those toils and storms of life into which it is entering. For as long as this life lasts there is effort and toil, nor unto them that undergo them can any consolations give more aid than those of patience.

We must endure and persevere, dearest brethren, that being admitted to the hope of truth and liberty, we may come even unto truth and liberty itself: for that same thing, that we are Christians, is a ground of faith and hope; but there is need of patience, that hope and faith may be made able to attain unto their fruit. For we follow present glory, as Paul the Apostle admonishes us and says, "We are saved by hope; but hope that is seen is not hope; for what a man seeth, why doth he hope? But if we hope for that we see not, then do we by patience wait for it." Wherefore waiting and patience are necessary, that we may fulfil that which we have begun to be, and that what we believe and hope for, we may when God gives it, receive. And in another place, the divine Apostle instructs and teaches the righteous and them that exercise good works, and that lay up for themselves heavenly treasures in the increase of the divine usury, to be patient likewise, saying, "Wherefore while we have time, let us do good unto all men, especially unto them who are of the household of faith. But let us not faint in well doing; for in due season we shall reap." He admonishes that no man through impatience faint in doing good; that no man, either called aside or overcome by temptations divert from the middle path of praise and glory, and the things that have been done be lost, in that those which had been begun cease to be brought to perfection. As it is written, "The righteousness of the righteous shall not deliver him, in the day when he shall transgress" (Ezek. xxxiii. 12.). And again, "Hold that which thou hast, that another take not thy crown" (Rev. iii. 11.). This voice admonishes us to persevere in patience and strength, so that he who now presses unto the crown with praise near to time, may become crowned through the continuance of patience.

But patience, dearest brethren, not only preserves what is good, but also repels what is evil. Accordant to the Holy Spirit, and blending with what is heavenly and divine, it wrestles by the resistance of its powers against those works of the flesh and body, by which the soul is overcome and captured. Let us now consider a few things from among many that from those few the others also may be understood. Adultery, fraud, murder, are mortal crimes. Let patience be strong and stedfast in the heart, and then neither is the sanctified body a Temple of God polluted with adultery; nor that innocence which had been dedicated to righteousness stained with the contagion of deceit; nor the hand which has carried the Eucharist, spotted with sword and bloodshed. Charity is the bond of brotherhood, the foundation of peace, the link and strength of unity; it is greater than both hope and faith; it has precedence both of good works and martyrdoms; it being eternal will evermore abide with us in God's Presence, in the realms of heaven. Take patience from it, and parted, it abides not. Take away the substance of bearing and enduring, and it has no root or strength to persevere withal. In fine, the Apostle when he spoke of charity, joined endurance and patience with it. "Charity," he says, "is of great soul, charity is kind, charity envieth not, is not puffed up, is not angered, thinketh no evil, is content with all things, believeth all things, hopeth all things, endureth all things." He shews that therefore it is able steadily to persevere, because it knows how to endure all things. And in another place he says, "Forbearing one another in love, endeavouring to keep the unity of the Spirit in the bond of peace." He shewed that neither unity nor peace can be preserved, unless brethren cherish one another with mutual long-suffering, and guard the band of concord by the mediation of patience.

How furthermore not to swear or curse; not to recover your goods taken from you; receiving a blow to turn the other cheek to the smiter; to forgive a brother that sins against you, not only seventy times seven, but altogether all his sins; to love your enemies, to offer prayer for your adversaries and persecutors: how shalt thou be able to fulfil these things except by stedfastness of patience and endurance? This we see fulfilled in Stephen, who when slain violently and with stones by the Jews, sought not revenge for himself, but pardon for his murderers, saying, "Lord, lay not this sin to their charge." Such was fittingly the first martyr of Christ, who, forerunning future martyrs in a glorious death, was not only preacher of the Passion of the Lord, but also the imitator of His most patient gentleness. What shall I say of anger, of discord, of hatred, which in a Christian ought not to be? Let but patience be in the breast, and these will not be able to find room within it; or if they attempt to enter, they are soon excluded and depart, that the house of peace may have continuance in a heart where it delights the God of peace to dwell. For if the Christian has gone forth from carnal rage and strife, as from among tempests of the sea, and is now entered tranquil and meek within the port of Christ, he should admit neither anger nor discord within his breast, for it is permitted here neither to render evil for evil, nor to bear hatred.

Furthermore, patience is needful for those various maladies of the flesh, frequent and hard pangs of the body, by which every day the human race is worn and shaken. For because in that first transgression of the commandment, strength of body departed together with immortality, and weakness came with death, and strength cannot be recovered until immortality is recovered, therefore there must needs be in this frailty and weakness of the body, a wrestling ever and a struggling, a wrestling and a struggling which cannot be undergone without strength from patience. And in this weighing and searching of us, manifold pains are applied, and varied kinds of trials are drawn down in the loss of professions, in the ardency of fevers, in the torture of wounds, and the bereavement of friends. Nor does any thing more distinguish between the unrighteous and the righteous than that the unrighteous in adversity complains and evil speaks through impatience, the righteous by patience is proved, as it is written, "In pain endure, and in thy low estate have patience, for gold and silver are tried in the fire" (Ecclus. ii. 4, 5.).

And, dearest brethren, that the blessedness of patience may the rather shine forth, let us consider on the other hand the mischief which impatience brings with it. For as patience is Christ's blessing, so impatience is the devil's curse; and as he in whom Christ dwells and abides is found patient, so he is ever impatient whose mind the devil's wickedness possesses. Whatever patience by its works builds up unto glory, impatience unbuilds unto ruin. Wherefore, dearest brethren, having diligently weighed both the benefits of patience, and the evils of impatience, let us hold fast in all observance that patience through which we abide in Christ in order that we may be able to come with Christ to God; patience, plenteous and manifold, not curtailed in a scanty course, nor straitened by contracted bounds.

The virtue of patience widely ranges, and its riches and largeness rising indeed in a fountain which has one name, flow out in gushing streams through many ways of glory; nor can any thing in our conduct avail for the perfecting of praise, except it take hence the substance of its perfection. It is patience which both commends and preserves us to God. It is this which restrains anger, bridles the tongue, governs the mind, guards peace, regulates discipline, breaks the impulse of lusts, binds down the violence of pride, quenches the flame of hatred, controls the power of the rich, comforts the wants of the poor, maintains a blessed integrity in virgins, in widows a studious chastity, in the wedded and married a singleness of love, makes men humble in prosperity, brave in adversity, mild towards injuries and contempts, teaches quickly to pardon them that offend; teaches the offender to make entreaty long and often; conquers temptations, bears persecutions, leads passions and martyrdoms to their consummation. It is this that firmly fortifies the foundations of our faith; it is this that bears upward the growings of our hope; this guides our conduct, that we may be able to hold the way of Christ, while we walk according to

His Long-suffering; and makes us to continue sons of God, by imitating the patience of our Father.

De Pat. II. xiv.

Wednesday in Passion Week.

ON HUMILITY. S. CHRYSOSTOM.

How shall a man find grace with God? How else, except by lowliness of mind? For "God," saith one, "resisteth the proud, but giveth grace unto the humble," (S. James iv. 6;) and, "the sacrifice of God is a broken spirit, and a heart that is brought low God will not despise." (Ps. li. 17.) For if with men humility is so lovely, much more with God. Thus both they of the Gentiles found grace, and the Jews no other way fell from grace; "for they were not subject unto the righteousness of God." (Rom. x. 3.) The lowly man of whom I am speaking is pleasing and delightful to all men, and dwells in continual peace, and hath in him no ground for contentions. For though you insult him, though you abuse him, whatsoever you say, he will be silent, and will bear it meekly, and will have so great peace towards all men as one cannot even describe. Yea, and with God also. For the commandments of God are to be at peace with men: and thus our whole life is made prosperous, through peace one with another. For no man can injure God: His Nature is imperishable, and above all suffering. Nothing makes the Christian so admirable as lowliness of mind. Hear for instance Abraham saying, "But I am but dust and ashes." (Gen. xviii. 27.) And again God saying of Moses that "he was the meekest of all men." (Numbers xii. 3.) For nothing was ever more humble than he; who being leader of so great a people, and having overwhelmed in the sea the king and all the host of the Egyptians, as if they had been flies; and having wrought so many wonders both in Egypt and by the Red Sea, and in the wilderness, and received such high testimony, yet felt exactly as if he had been an ordinary person, and as a son-in-law, was humbler than his father-in-law, and took advice from him, (Exod. xviii. 24,) and was not indignant, nor did he say, "What is this? After such and so great achievements, art thou come to us with thy counsel?" This is what most people feel, though a man bring the best advice, despising it, because of the lowliness of the person. But not so did he: rather through lowliness of mind he wrought all things well. Hence also he despised the courts of kings, since he was lowly indeed: for the sound and high spirit are the fruit of humility. For of how great nobleness and magnanimity thinkest thou, were it a token, to despise the kingly palace and table? since kings among the Egyptians are honoured as gods, and enjoy wealth and treasures inexhaustible. But nevertheless, letting go all these, and throwing away the very sceptres of Egypt, he hastened to join himself unto captives, and men worn down with toil, whose strength was spent in the clay and the making of bricks, men whom his own slaves abhorred, for saith he, "The Egyptians abhorred them," (Ex. i. 2; Sept.,) unto these he ran, and preferred them before their masters. From whence it is plain, that whoso is lowly, the same is high and great of soul. For as pride cometh of an ordinary mind and an ignoble spirit; so moderation of a temper meet for high purposes and high thoughts.

And if you please, let us try both by certain examples. For tell me, what was there ever more exalted than Abraham? And yet it was he that said, "I am but dust and ashes:" it was he who said, "Let there be no strife between me and thee." (Gen. xiii. 8.) But this man so humble, despised Persian spoils, and regarded not barbaric trophies; (Gen. xiv. 21—24;) and this he did of much highmindedness, and of a spirit nobly nurtured. For he is indeed exalted who is truly humble; (not the flatterer nor the dissembler;) for true greatness is one thing, and arrogance another. And this is plain, from hence: if one man esteem clay to be clay, and despise it, and another admire the clay as gold, and account it a great thing, which, I ask, is the man of exalted mind? Is it not he who refuses to admire the clay? And which abject and mean? Is it not he who admires it and sets much store by it? Just so do thou esteem of this case also; that he who calls himself but dust and ashes is exalted, although he say it out of humility; but that he who does not consider himself dust and ashes, but treats himself lovingly, and has high thoughts, this man for his part must be counted mean, esteeming little things to be great. Whence it is clear that out of great loftiness of thought the patriarch spoke that saying, "I am but dust and ashes:" from loftiness of thought, not from arrogance.

For as in bodies it is one thing to be healthy and plump, and another thing to be swoln, although both are betokened by a full habit of flesh, (but in this case of unsound, in that of healthful flesh;) so also here: it is one thing to be arrogant, which is as it were to be swoln, and another thing to be high-souled, which is to be in a healthy state. And again, one man is tall from the stature of his person; another being short, by adding buskins becomes taller; now tell me which of the two should we call tall and large? Is it not quite plain, him whose height is from himself? For the other has it as something not his own, and stepping upon things low in themselves, turns out a tall person. Such is the case with many men who mount themselves up on wealth and glory; which is not exaltation, for he is exalted who wants none of these things, but despises them, and has his greatness from himself. Let us therefore become humble that we may become exalted; "for he that humbleth himself shall be exalted." (St. Luke xiv. 11.) Now the self-willed man is not such as this; rather he is of all characters the most ordinary. For the bubble too is inflated, but the inflation is not sound: wherefore we call these persons "puffed up." Whereas the sober-minded man has no high thoughts, not even in high fortunes, knowing his own low estate; but the vulgar even in his trifling concerns indulges in a proud fancy.

Let us then acquire that height which comes by humility. Let us look into the nature of human things, that we may kindle with the longing desire of the things to come; for in no other way is it possible to become humble, except by the love of what is divine, and the contempt of what is present. For just as a man on the point of obtaining a kingdom, if instead of that purple robe one offer him some trivial compliment, will count it to be nothing; so shall we also laugh to scorn all things present, if we desire that other sort of honour. Do ye not see the children, when in their play they make a band of soldiers, and heralds precede them, and lictors, and a boy marches in the midst in the general's place, how childish it all is? Just such are all human affairs; yea, and more worthless than these: to-day they are, and to-morrow they are not. Let us therefore be above these things; and let us not only not desire them, but even be ashamed if any one hold them forth to us. For thus casting out the love of these things, we shall possess that other love which is divine, and shall enjoy immortal glory. Which may God grant us all to obtain, through the grace and loving-kindness of our Lord Jesus Christ.

In Cor. Hom. i.

Thursday in Passion Week.

TRUE WISDOM. S. CHRYSOSTOM.
1 Cor. ii. 6, 7.

DARKNESS seems to be more suitable than light to those that are diseased in their eye-sight: wherefore they betake themselves by preference to some room that is thoroughly shaded over. This also is the case with the wisdom that is spiritual. As the wisdom which is of God seemed to be foolishness unto those without; so their own wisdom, being foolishness indeed, was accounted by them wisdom. The result has been, just as if a man having skill in navigation, were to promise that without a ship or sails he would pass over a boundless tract of the sea, and then endeavour by reasonings to prove that the thing is possible; but some other person ignorant of it all, committing himself to a ship and a steersman, and to sailors, were thus to sail in safety. For the seeming ignorance of this man is wiser than the wisdom of the other. For excellent is the art of managing a ship; but when it makes too great professions, it is a kind of folly. And so is every art which is not contented with its own proper limits. Just so the wisdom which is without were wisdom indeed, if it had the benefit of the Spirit. But since it trusted all to itself, and supposed that it wanted none of that help, it became foolishness, although it seemed to be wisdom. Wherefore having first exposed it by the facts, then and not till then the Apostle calls it foolishness, and having first called the wisdom of God folly, according to their reckoning, then and not till then he shews it to be wisdom. His words then are, "Howbeit, we speak wisdom among them which are perfect:" for when I, accounted as I am foolish, and a preacher of follies, get the better of the wise, I overcome wisdom, not by foolishness, but by a more perfect wisdom; a wisdom too so ample, and so much greater, that the other appears foolishness.

"Wisdom" is the name he gives to the Gospel, to the method of salvation, the being saved by the Cross. "The perfect" are those that believe. For indeed they are perfect who know all human things, that they are utterly helpless, and who overlook them from conviction, that by such they are profited nothing: such as were the true believers.

"But not the wisdom of this world." For where is the use of the wisdom which is without, terminating here, and proceeding no further, and not even here able to profit its possessors?

Now by "the princes of this world," here he means those in authority, those in power, those who esteem the things worth contending about, philosophers, rhetoricians and orators. For these were the dominant sort, and often became leaders of the people.

"Rulers of this world" he calls them, because

beyond this present world their dominion extends not. Wherefore he adds further, " Which come to nought;" disparaging it both on its own account, and from those who wield it. For having shewn that it is false, that it is foolish, that it is unable to discover any thing, that it is weak, he shews moreover that it is but of short duration.

" But we speak the wisdom of God in a mystery." What mystery ? For surely Christ saith, " What ye have heard in the ear, proclaim upon the house-tops." How then does he call it a *mystery ?* Because that neither angel nor archangel, nor any other created power knew of it before it actually took place. Wherefore he saith, " That now unto the principalities and powers in heavenly places might be known by the Church the manifold wisdom of God." And this hath God done in honour to us, so that they not without us should hear the mysteries. For we too ourselves, whomsoever we make our friends, use to speak of this as a sure proof of friendship towards them, that we tell our secrets to no one in preference to them. Let those hear who make a sort of triumphal show of the secrets of the Gospel, and unto all indiscriminately display the pearls and the doctrine, and who cast the holy things unto dogs and swine, and useless reasonings. For the mystery wants no adornment; but just what the fact is, that it is simply declared to be, since it will not be a mystery divine and whole in all its parts, when thou addest any thing to it of thyself also.

And in another sense too a mystery is so called,

because we believe not the very things which we see, but some things we see and others believe. For such is the nature of our mysteries. I for instance feel differently upon these subjects from an unbeliever. I hear, " Christ was crucified:" and forthwith I admire His loving-kindness unto men; the other hears and esteems it weakness. I hear, " He became a servant:" and I wonder at the care which He hath had for us; the other hears and counts it dishonour. I hear, "He died;" and am astonished at His might, that being in death He was not holden, but even broke the bonds of death; the other hears, and surmises it to be helplessness. He hearing of the Resurrection, saith, the thing is a legend; I, aware of the facts which demonstrate it, fall down and worship the economy of God. He hearing of a laver, counts it merely as water; but I behold not simply the thing which is seen, but the purification of the soul which is by the Spirit. He considers only that my body hath been washed; but I believe that the soul also hath become both pure and holy; and I count it the Sepulchre, the Resurrection, the Sanctification, the Righteousness, the Redemption, the Adoption, the Inheritance, the Kingdom of heaven, the plenary effusion of the Spirit. For not by the sight do I judge of the things that appear, but by the eyes of the mind. I hear of the Body of Christ: in one sense I understand the expression, in another sense the unbeliever.

And just as children, looking on their books, know not the meaning of the letters, neither know what they see; yea more, if even a grown man be unskilful in letters the same thing will befall him; but the skilful will find much meaning stored up in the letters, even complete lines and histories: and an epistle in the hands of one that is unskilful, will be accounted but paper and ink, but he that knows how to read will both hear a voice, and hold converse with the absent, and will reply whatsoever he chooses by means of writing; so it is also in regard of the mystery. Unbelievers albeit they seem to hear, hear not; but the faithful, having the skill which is by the Spirit, behold the meaning of the things stored therein. For instance, it is this very thing that Paul signified, when he said that even now the word preached is hidden: for "unto them that perish," he saith, "it is hidden."

By the name of Wisdom, he calls both Christ and the Cross and the Gospel. Opportunely also he called Him, "the Lord of glory." For seeing that the Cross is counted a matter of ignominy, he signifies that the Cross was great glory; but that there was need of great wisdom in order to join with the knowledge of God the learning of this, God's dispensation: and the wisdom which was without turned out an obstacle, not to the former only but to the latter also.

What then, hath "eye not seen what God hath prepared?" No, for who among men saw the things which were about to be dispensed? Hath then "ear not heard? neither hath it entered into the heart of man?" How is this? For if the prophets spoke of it, how saith he, "ear hath not heard?" The prophet truly heard, but not with the ear of man; for not as men heard they, but as prophets. And so by what is esteemed to be the foolishness of preaching, He shall overcome the world and the nations shall be brought in, and there shall be reconciliation of God with men, and so great blessings shall come upon us.

In 1 Cor. Hom. vii.

Friday in Passion Week.

TRIBULATION. S. AUGUSTINE.

"WOE unto the world because of offences." Now I would say a few words about offences, of which the world is full, and how it is that offences thicken, pressing troubles abound. The world is laid waste, the wine-press is trodden. Ah Christians! heavenly shoot, ye strangers on the earth, who seek a city in heaven, who long to be associated with the holy angels; understand that ye have come here on this condition only, that ye should soon depart. Ye are passing on through the world endeavouring to reach Him Who created it. Let not the lovers of the world, who wish to remain in the world, and yet whether they will or no, are compelled to move from it; let them not disturb you, let them not deceive nor seduce you. These pressing troubles are not offences. Be ye righteous, and they will be only exercises. Tribulation comes; it will be as ye choose it, either an exercise, or a condemnation. Such as it shall find you to be, will it be. Tribulation is a fire: does it find thee gold? it takes away the filth: does it find thee chaff? it turns it into ashes. The pressing troubles then which abound are not *offences*. But what are *offences?* Those expressions, those words in which we are thus addressed: "See what Christian times bring about." Lo, these are the true offences. For this is said to thee, to this end, that if thou love the world, thou mayest blaspheme Christ. And this he saith to thee who is thy friend and counsellor; and so thine *eye*. This he saith to thee who ministereth to thee, and shareth thy labours, and so thine *hand*. This he saith to thee it may be who supporteth thee, who lifteth thee up from a low earthly state, and so thy *foot*. Cast them all aside, cut them off, throw them all away from thee; consent not unto them. Answer such men as he who was advised to give false witness answered. So do thou answer too; say to the man who saith to thee, "See, it is in Christian times that there are such pressing troubles; that the whole world is laid waste;" answer him, "And this Christ foretold me, before it came to pass."

For wherefore art thou disturbed? Thine heart is disturbed by the pressing troubles of the world, as that ship was in which Christ was asleep. Lo!

what is the cause, stout-hearted man, that thy heart is disturbed? That ship in which Christ is asleep is the heart in which faith is asleep. For what new thing, what new thing, I ask, is told thee, Christian? Did not thy Lord tell thee the world shall be laid waste? Did not thy Lord tell thee the world should fail? Why when the promise was made didst thou believe, and art disturbed now, when it is being completed? So then the tempest beats furiously against thine heart; beware of shipwreck, awake up Christ. The Apostle says, "that Christ may dwell in your hearts by faith." Christ dwelleth in thee by faith. Present faith is Christ present, waking faith is Christ awake, slumbering faith is Christ asleep. Arise and stir thyself; say, "Lord, we perish." See what the unbelievers say to us; and what is worse, what evil Christians say. "Awake up, O Lord, we perish." Let thy faith awake, and Christ begins to speak to thee. "Why art thou troubled?" I told thee beforehand of all these things. I foretold them, that when evils came, thou mightest hope for good things, that thou mightest not faint in the evil. Wonderest thou that the world is failing? Wonder that the world is grown old. It is as a man who is born and grows up, and waxes old. There are many complaints in old age; the coughs, the rheum, weakness of the eyes, fretfulness and weariness. So then as when a man is old he is full of complaints, so is the world old, and is full of troubles. Is it a little thing that God hath done for thee, that in the world's old age He hath sent Christ unto thee, that He may renew thee then, when all is failing? Therefore was a son born to Abraham in his old age, because in the old age of this world was Christ to come. He came when all things were growing old, and made them new. As a made, created, perishing thing, the world was now declining to its fall. It could not but be that it should abound in troubles; He came both to console thee in the midst of present troubles, and to promise thee everlasting rest. Choose not then to cleave to this aged world, and to be unwilling to grow young in Christ, Who telleth thee, the world is waxing old, the world is failing, is distressed by the breathing of old age. But do not thou fear, "Thy youth shall be renewed as the eagle's" (Ps. ciii. 5.).

Hom. on the New Test., xxxi.

Saturday in Passion Week.

UNITY. S. Chrysostom.

"Other foundation can no man lay than that which is laid." Upon this then let us build, and as a foundation let us cleave to it, as a branch to a vine; and let there be no interval between us and Christ. For if there be any interval, immediately we perish. For so the branch, by its adherence, draws in the fatness, and the building stands, because it is cemented together. Since if it stand apart, it perishes, having nothing whereon to support itself. Let us not then merely keep hold of Christ, but let us be joined unto Him, for if we stand apart, we perish. "For they who withdraw themselves far from Thee shall perish;" so it is said (Ps. lxxiii. 27. Sept.). Let us cleave then to Him, and let us cleave by our works. "For he that keepeth My commandments, the same abideth in Me" (St. John xiv. 21.). And accordingly there are many images, whereby He brings us into union. Thus if you mark it, He is the "Head," we are the body: can there be any interval between the head and the body? He is a Foundation, we the building; He a Vine, we branches; He the Bridegroom, we the bride; He the Shepherd, we the sheep; He is the Way, we "they who walk therein." Again, we are a temple, He the Indweller; He the First Begotten, we the brethren; He the Heir, we the "heirs together with Him;" He the Life, we the living; He the Resurrection, we "those who rise again;" He the Light, we the enlightened. All these things indicate unity, and they allow no void interval, not even the smallest. For he that removes but to a little distance, will go on till he has become very far distant. For so the body, receiving though it be but a small cut by a sword, perishes; and the building, though there be but a small chink, falls to decay; and the branch, though it be but a little while cut off from the root, becomes useless. So that this trifle is no trifle, but is even almost the whole.

In Cor. Hom. viii.

Palm Sunday.

THE CHRISTIAN'S HOPE. S. Augustine.

"We are saved in hope, but hope that is seen is not hope; for what a man seeth, why doth he hope for? But if we hope for that we see not, then do we with patience wait for it." The Lord our God Himself, to Whom it is said in the Psalm, "Thou art my hope and my portion in the land of the living," admonisheth me to give you hereupon some words of exhortation and consolation. He Himself, I say, "Who is our hope in the land of the living," enjoineth me to address you in this land of the dying; that ye may not "look at the things which are seen, but at the things which are not seen. For the things which are seen are temporal but the things which are not seen are eternal." Because then we "hope for that we see not, and with patience wait for it," with good reason it is said to us in the Psalm, "Wait patiently on the Lord, do manfully, and let thy heart take courage, yea wait patiently on the Lord." (Ps. xxvii. 14. Sept.) For the world's promises are always deceiving, but the promises of God never deceive. But because the world seems as if ready to give what it promises here, that is, in this land of the dying, wherein we now are; but God will give what He promiseth, " in the land of the living ;" many are wearied of waiting patiently for the True, and blush not to love the deceitful one. Of such the Scripture saith, " Woe unto them that have lost patience, and have turned aside into crooked ways." (Ecclus. ii. 14.) With those who do manfully, and with heart of good courage wait patiently on the Lord, the children of eternal death also cease not to mock, vaunting their transitory delights, which for a time are sweet to their mouths, but afterwards they shall find them more bitter than gall. For they say unto us, " Where is that that is promised you after this life? who hath returned hither from thence, and given information that the things ye believe are true? lo, we joy in the fulness of our pleasures, in that we hope for what we see; but ye are tormented in the travails of self-denial, by believing what ye do not see." And then they subjoin the words the Apostle brought forward : " Let us eat and drink, for to-morrow we shall die." But see what he advised us to beware of. " Evil communications," saith he, " corrupt good manners. Be ye sober in righteousness, and sin not."

Beware then, brethren, lest by such communications your manners be corrupted, hope overthrown, patience enfeebled, and ye turn aside into crooked ways. Yea rather in meekness and gentleness hold on the strait ways, which the Lord teacheth you ; of whom the Psalm saith, " The meek shall He direct in judgment, the gentle shall He teach His ways." Patience indeed among the toils of this life, without which the hope of the Life to come cannot be maintained, can no one retain continually, but the meek and gentle, who resisteth not the Will of God, "Whose yoke is easy and His burden light," but only to those who believe in God, who hope in Him, and love Him. So truly as meek and gentle ye will not only love His consolations, but as good children ye will also endure His scourges; that since ye hope for that ye see not, ye may with patience wait for it. So act, so walk ye. For so ye walk in Christ Who said, "I am the Way." How you must walk in Him, learn, not only by His Word, but also by His example. For this "His Own Son the Father spared not, but delivered Him up for us all;" not of course against His will, not refusing, but equally willing with the Father; for that the will of the Father and the Son is One in His Equality in "the Form of God, Being," in which "He thought it not robbery to be equal with God," and pre-eminently obedient, in His "emptying of Himself, taking the form of a servant. For He Himself loved us, and gave Himself up for us an offering and a Sacrifice to God for an odour of sweetness." In such wise then "the Father spared not His own Son, but delivered Him up for us all," as that the Son Himself also delivered Himself up for us.

He then the High One, "by Whom all things were made," being delivered up, by reason of the form of a servant delivered up to the reproach of men, and the despising of the people, to contumely, to scourging, to the death of the Cross, hath taught us by the example of His Resurrection what we ought in patience to hope from Him. "For if we hope for that we see not, then do we with patience wait for it." We hope, it is true, for that we see not; but we are the Body of that Head, in Whom what we hope for hath already been perfected. For of Him it is said, that "He is the Head of the Body, the Church, the First Begotten, holding Himself the pre-eminence." And of us it is written, "Now we are the Body of Christ and members; now if we hope for that we see not, then do we with patience wait for it," in firm assurance, since He Who hath risen is our Head, He reserveth our hope. And in that before He rose again, our Head was scourged, He hath confirmed our patience. For it is written, "Whom the Lord loveth He chasteneth, and scourgeth every son whom He receiveth." Let us not then faint under the scourge, that we may rejoice in the Resurrection. For so true is it that He scourgeth every son whom He receiveth, that "He spared not even His Only Son, but delivered Him up for us all." Looking then at Him, Who without the desert of sin was scourged, "Who died for our sins, and rose again for our justification," let us not fear lest we be cast away when we have been scourged, but rather let us believe that we shall be received, having been justified. For although the fulness of our joy be not yet come; yet not even now have we been left without joy; for "we are saved in hope." Accordingly the Apostle himself too, who saith, "If we hope for that we see not, then do we with patience wait for it ;" saith in another place, "Rejoicing in hope, patient in tribulation. Having then such hope, let us use much confidence; and let our speech in grace be seasoned with salt, that we may know how we ought to answer every one." For we must say to them, who since they have lost, or have never received patience, dare even to insult, whereas they ought to imitate us who wait patiently on the Lord, (because hoping for that we see not, we do in patience wait for it,) "Where are your delights, for which ye walk in crooked ways?" We do not say, "Where shall they be, when this life hath passed away?" but where are they now? When to-day has removed yesterday, and to-morrow is about to remove to-day, what is there of the things ye love that does not flit, and fly away? What is there that does not fly away almost before it is taken, since of this very to-day, not even an hour can be retained? For so the second is shut out by the third, just as the first was by the second. Of this very one hour, which seems present, nothing is present: for all its portions, and all its moments are fleeting.

What man sins for, if he be not thoroughly blinded when he sins, let him at least, now he hath sinned, give heed. He might see that pleasure that is to pass away is without any wisdom longed for: or when it is passed away, is with repentance thought of. Ye laugh at us, because we hope for things eternal, which we do not see; whereas ye, enchained to those temporal things which are seen, know not what kind of day to-morrow's sun will bring you:

Q

which when ye hope to be good, ye often find evil; nor if it shall be good, will ye be able to hold it that it fly not away. Ye laugh at us because we hope for things eternal; which when they come shall not pass away; because they do not even come, but abide ever; but we shall come to them, when by the way of the Lord we shall have passed over those things which pass away. But by you these temporal things never cease to be hoped for, and yet the things ye hope for frequently deceive you; nor do they cease to inflame you when they are yet to come, to corrupt when they come, to torment when they pass away. Are they not things which when coveted kindle hot desires, obtained are disesteemed, lost vanish into nothing? We too make use of them as the necessity of this pilgrim state requires, but we do not fix our joys in them, lest we be overwhelmed with them when they fall. For we "use this world as not using it," that we may come to Him Who made this world, and abide in Him, enjoying His eternity.

But what is it that ye say, "Who hath come hither from thence, and who hath informed men of what is passing among the dead?" On this point too hath He shut your mouth, Who rose again a dead man on the fourth day, and on the third day rose again. Himself, now to die no more, and before He died, told us, as He from Whom nothing could be hid, in the narrative of the beggar at rest, and the rich man in flames, what sort of life receives those who die. But these things they do not believe, who say, Who hath returned hither from thence? They wish it to be thought they would believe, if one of their own ancestors were to return to life. But " cursed is every one who putteth his hope in man." (Jer. xvii. 5.) For this reason then God, made Man, was pleased to die and rise again, that both what was to happen to man might be shewed him in man's flesh, and yet that belief might be had in God, not in man. And at all events the Church of the faithful, spread over the whole world, is now before their eyes. Let them read of it promised so many ages before to one man, " who against hope believed in hope, that he might become the father of many nations." What then was promised to one man, Abraham believing, we see now fulfilled; and do not despair of that coming which is promised to the whole world believing? Let them go now and say, " Let us eat and drink for to-morrow we shall die." They are still saying that they are to die to-morrow, but when they use such language, the Truth findeth them dead already. But ye, brethren, children of the Resurrection, citizens with the holy angels, heirs of God, and joint heirs with Christ, beware ye of imitating those who die to-morrow in breathing out their last, and are buried in sin to-day. But as the same Apostle saith, " Let not evil communications corrupt your good manners, be ye sober·in righteousness, and sin not;" walking the narrow road, but the certain way which leadeth to the expanse of the heavenly Jerusalem, which is our eternal mother; hope in firmest assurance for that ye see not, wait patiently for that ye have not yet; for that ye hold Christ the True Promiser as a most sure guarantee.

Homil. on the New Testament, cvii.

Monday in Holy Week.

FEAR OF DEATH. S. CYPRIAN.

LET him fear to die, and only him, who, unborn of water and of the Spirit, is the property of hell-fire; let him fear to die who is without title in the Cross and Passion of Christ; let him fear to die who is to pass from death here into the second death; let him fear to die, on whom at his going away from life, an eternal flame will lay pains that never cease; let him fear to die on whom the longer delay confers this boon, that his tortures and groans will begin the later.

We should remember that we ought to do, not our own will, but the Will of God; according as the Lord has commanded us daily to pray. How misplaced is it, and how perverse, while we make it our prayer that the Will of God may be done, yet when God calls and withdraws us from this world, not at once to obey the requirements of His Will! We oppose and withstand, and after the manner of contumacious servants we are carried into the presence of our

Lord with reluctance and sadness, departing hence under the constraint of necessity, not the obedience of choice; and desire to be honoured of Him with heavenly rewards, Whom we approach against our will? Why then do we pray and beseech that the kingdom of heaven may come, if bondage on earth delights us? Why in oft repeated prayers do we inquire and ask that the day of the kingdom may hasten, when we desire and have it rather in our wish to serve the devil here, than to be reigning with Christ?

Neither ought we to sorrow for those our brethren, who by the Lord's summons have been set at liberty from the life below; assured that they are not gone away, but gone forward; that in departing from us they are but leading the way, as is men's wont in a journey or upon a voyage; that we owe them our affection rather than our lamentations; and ought not to put on the garb of black here, while they have already taken on them white raiment there; since occasion must not be given to the Gentiles for the deserved and just reproach, that while we say of men, they are alive with God, we mourn for them as extinct and perished; and that a faith which we manifest by language and utterance, is disproved in the testimony of our feeling and thoughts.

So doing we play false to our hope and faith; unreal, counterfeit, fictitious do these things appear which we affirm. It nothing profits to set out virtue in our words, in our acts to undo the truth. In a word, the Apostle Paul condemns and rebukes and blames any who sorrow at the departing of them who are dear to them. "I would not," says he, "have you ignorant, brethren, concerning them which are asleep, that ye sorrow not even as others which have no hope. For if we believe that Jesus died and rose again, even so them which are asleep in Jesus will God bring with Him." They, he says, sorrow in the departing of their friends, which have no hope. But we who live by hope, and believe in God, and are assured that Christ suffered for us, and that He rose again, abiding in Christ, and having resurrection by Him and in Him, wherefore do we either ourselves unwillingly depart forth from life, or lament and grieve for those of us who do depart, as though they perished? Christ Himself, our Lord and God, cautions us and says, "I am the Resurrection and the Life: he that believeth in Me, though he die, shall live; and whosoever liveth and believeth in Me shall not die eternally." If we believe in Christ, let us put faith in His words and promises; and since we shall not die eternally, let us pass in joyful assurance unto Christ, with Whom for ever we shall both live and reign. In dying at this present, by death gain the transit to immortality; eternal life cannot follow, unless it has been given us to depart hence; nor is this departure, but transition; when the journey of time is concluded, a transit unto things eternal. Who will not make speed unto the better things? Who does not long to be changed, and made anew unto the Likeness of Christ, and to gain an earlier entrance to the dignity of heavenly grace? It is the spoken word of Paul the Apostle; "Our conversation," saith he, "is in heaven; from whence also we look for the Lord Jesus Christ, Who shall change the body of our humility, conforming it to the body of His glory." That such we shall be, Christ the Lord also promises when in these words He prays the Father for us, that we may be with Him, and live with Him in the eternal seats, and be joyful in the realms of heaven. "Father, I will that they also whom Thou hast given Me, be with Me where I am; and may see the glory which Thou gavest Me before the world began."

He who is going to the seat of Christ, to the brightness of the heavenly kingdoms, ought not to weep and lament, but rather according to the promise of the Lord, according to his belief of the truth, to be joyful in this his departure and translation. Thus accordingly we find Enoch was translated, who pleased God, as divine Scripture bears witness, and speaks in Genesis: "And Enoch pleased God and he was not found after, because God translated him." His having been found well-pleasing in the Sight of God, wrought for him a translation out of this infectious world. Thus also the Holy Spirit teacheth by Solomon, that they who please God are earlier taken hence, more speedily set free; lest abiding longer in this world they are polluted by its contact with them. "He was taken away," saith he, "lest that wickedness should alter his understanding, for his soul pleased God; wherefore hasted He to take him away from the midst of wickedness." Then also in the Psalms, the soul devoted in spiritual faith unto its God, makes haste unto the Lord, saying, "How amiable are Thy Tabernacles, O God of Hosts! My soul longeth and hasteth unto the courts of God." It is for him to wish to remain long below, who finds below his enjoyment, whom a flattering and deceiving world attracts by the enticement of earthly pleasure.

Furthermore, whereas the world hates the Christian, wherefore love that which hates thee? and not rather follow Christ, Who hath redeemed and loves thee? John in his Epistle cries out and says, warning us that we be not made lovers of the world, while we indulge in carnal desires, "Love not the world, neither the things that are in the world: if any man love the world, the Love of the Father is not in him; for all that is in the world is lust of the flesh, and lust of the eyes, and pride of life; which is not of the Father, but of the lust of the world; and the world will pass away and the lust thereof; but he that doeth the Will of God abideth for ever, even as God abideth for ever." Rather, dearest brethren, in fulness of spirit, firm faith, and hearty courage, let us be prepared unto all the Will of God, shutting out our dread of death, and thinking of the deathlessness which comes beyond it. Herein let us manifest that we live as we believe; on the one hand, by not lamenting the departure of them we love; and on the other, when the day of our own summons comes, by going without delay, and with a ready mind, unto the Lord Who calls us.

Even as the servants of God ought thus to do, now ought they to do so much more, in a world which has begun to crumble, and is beset with storms of harassing calamity; for seeing ill things are begun, and since we know that worse are impending, we ought to account it our greatest gain, to take our departure hence the sooner. If the walls of your mansion were tottering with age, the roof shaking above you, and the edifice, wasted and wearied out, threatening an instant ruin of its time-enfeebled structure, would you not in all haste go forth from it? If when you were on a voyage a swelling and troublous tempest tossed up the waves in its strength, and betokened impending shipwreck, would you not hurry forward to the port? See a world tottering and going down, witnessing to its own dissolution, not merely in the old age of things, but in their conclusions, and thank you not God, are you not rejoiced, that escaping by an earlier removal, you are rescued from overhanging ruins and shipwrecks and plagues?

We ought to consider, dearest brethren, we ought indeed to retain in our meditations, that we have renounced the world, and are continuing here, for this mean season, as strangers and pilgrims. Let us embrace the day which makes over each of us to his own resting place, which after rescuing us hence, and ridding us of the chains of earth, places us back in Paradise, and in the heavenly kingdom. What man that is journeying abroad, doth not hasten backward to his native land? Who that is speeding a voyage towards them he loves, longs not with more ardour for a prosperous wind, that so he may embrace his friends the sooner? Paradise we are to reckon for our native land; Patriarchs are now our parents: wherefore not haste and run to behold our country, to salute our parents? It is a large and loving company who expect us there, parents, brothers, children, a manifold and numerous assemblage longing after us, who having security of their own immortality, still feel anxiety for our salvation. What a common gladness, both to them and us, when we pass into their presence and their embrace! And O sweet heavenly realms, where death can never terrify, and life can never end! Ah perfect and perpetual bliss! There is the glorious company of the Apostles; there is the assembly of Prophets exulting; there is the innumerable multitude of Martyrs crowned after their victory of strife and passion; there are virgins triumphant, who have overcome all earthly passions; there are merciful men, obtaining mercy, who fulfilled the works of righteousness by dealing food and bounty to the poor, and in obedience to the instructions of the Lord translated the inheritance of earth into the treasuries of heaven. To these, dearest brethren, let us with eager longings hasten; let it be the portion which we desire, speedily to be among them, speedily to be gone to Christ: God behold this thought of ours! this purpose of our mind and faith may the Lord Jesus Christ witness, Who will make the recompences of His glory the larger according as man's longings after Him have been the stronger. De Mortalit.

Tuesday in Holy Week.

THE CROSS OF CHRIST. S. Chrysostom.

Let no man be ashamed of the honoured symbols of our salvation, and of the chiefest of all good things, whereby we even live, and whereby we are; but as a crown, so let us bear about the Cross of Christ, yea, for by it all things are wrought that are wrought among us. Whether one is to be new-born, the Cross is there; or to be nourished with that Mystical Food, or to be ordained, or to do any thing else, everywhere our symbol of victory is present. Therefore both upon our house and walls, and windows, and upon our forehead, and upon our mind, we inscribe it with much care.

For of the salvation wrought for us, and of our common freedom, and of the goodness of our Lord, this is the sign. "For as a sheep was He led to the slaughter." When therefore thou signest thyself, think of the purpose of the Cross, and quench anger and all the other passions. When thou signest thyself, fill thy forehead with all courage, make thy soul free. And ye know assuredly what are the things that give freedom. Wherefore also Paul leading us there, I mean unto the freedom that beseems us, did on this wise lead us unto it, having reminded us of the Cross and Blood of our Lord. "For ye are bought," saith he, "with a price; be not ye the servants of men." Consider, saith he, the price that hath been paid for thee, and thou wilt be a slave to no man; by the price meaning the Cross. Since not merely by the fingers ought one to engrave it, but before this by the purpose of the heart with much faith. And if in this way thou hast marked it on thy face, none of the unclean spirits will be able to stand near thee, seeing the blade whereby he received his wound, seeing the sword which gave him his mortal stroke. For if we, on seeing the place in which the criminals are beheaded, shudder; think what the devil must endure, seeing the weapon whereby Christ put an end to all his power, and cut off the head of the dragon.

Be not ashamed then of so great a blessing, lest Christ be ashamed of thee, when He comes with His glory, and the sign appears before Him, shining beyond the very sunbeam. For indeed the Cross cometh then, uttering a voice by its appearance, and pleading with the whole world for our Lord, and signifying that no part hath failed of what pertained to Him.

This therefore do thou engrave upon thy mind, and embrace the salvation of our souls. For this Cross saved and converted the world, drove away error, brought back truth, made earth heaven, fashioned men into angels. Because of this, the devils are no longer terrible, but contemptible; neither is death death, but a sleep; because of this, all that warreth against us is cast to the ground, and trodden under foot.

If any one therefore say to thee, Dost thou worship the Crucified? say with your voice all joy, and your countenance gladdened, I do both worship Him, and will never cease to worship; and so let us with a clear voice, shouting both loud and high, cry out and say, that the Cross is our glory, and the sum of all our blessings, and our confidence, and all our crown. I would that also with Paul I were able to say, "By which the world is crucified unto me, and I unto the world!" but I cannot, restrained as I am by various passions.

Wherefore I admonish both you, and surely before you myself, to be crucified to the world, and to have nothing in common with the earth, but to set your love on your country above, and the glory and the good things that come from it. For indeed we are soldiers of a heavenly King, and are clad with spiritual arms. Why then take we upon ourselves the life of traders, and mountebanks, nay rather of worms? For where the King is, there should also the soldier be. Yea we are become soldiers, not of them that are far off, but of them that are near. For the earthly king indeed would not endure that all should be in the royal courts, and at his own side, but the King of the heavens willeth all to be near His Royal Throne.

And how, one may say, is it possible for us, being here, to stand by that Throne? Because Paul too, being on earth, was where the Seraphim, where the

Cherubim are; and nearer to Christ than these the body guards to the king. For these turn about their faces in many directions, but him nothing beguiled nor distracted, but he kept his whole mind intent upon the King. So that if we would, this is possible to us also.

⟨For were He distant from us in place, thou mightest well doubt, but if He is present everywhere, to him that strives and is in earnest He is near.⟩ Wherefore also the Prophet said, "I will fear no evil, for Thou art with me;" and God Himself again, "I am a God nigh at hand, and not a God afar off." Then as our sins separate us from Him, so do our righteousnesses draw us nigh unto Him, "For while thou art yet speaking," it is said, "I will say, Here I am." (Isa. lviii. 9; lxv. 24.) What father would ever be thus obedient to his offspring? What mother is there, so ready and continually standing, if haply her children call her? There is not one, no father, no mother; but God stands continually waiting, if any of His servants should perchance call Him; and never when we have called as we ought, hath He refused to hear. Therefore He saith, "While thou art yet speaking," I do not wait for thee to finish, and I straightway hearken.

Let us call Him therefore, as it is His Will to be called. And what is this His Will? "Loose," saith He, "every band of iniquity, unloose the twisted knots of oppressive covenants, tear in pieces every unjust contract. Break thy bread to the hungry, and bring in the poor that are cast out to thy house. If thou seest one naked, cover him, and them that belong to thy seed thou shalt not overlook. Then shall thy light break forth as the morning, and thy healings shall spring forth speedily, and thy righteousness shall go before thee, and the glory of the Lord shall cover thee. Then thou shalt call upon Me, and I will give ear unto thee; whilst thou art yet speaking, I will say, Lo! here I am." (Is. lviii. 6—9.)

And who is able to do all this? it may be asked. Nay who is unable, I pray thee? For which is difficult of the things I have mentioned? Which is laborious? Which not easy? Why so entirely are they not possible only, but even easy, that many have actually overshot the measure of those sayings, not only tearing in pieces unjust contracts, but even stripping themselves of all their goods; making the poor welcome, not only to roof and table, but even to the sweat of their brow, and labouring in order to maintain them; doing good not to kinsmen only, but even to enemies. Let us also learn the meaning of "the light shall break forth." For He saith " shall break forth," declaring to us its quickness and plentifulness, and how exceedingly He desires our salvation; and how the good things themselves travail to come forth and press on; and that which would check their unspeakable force shall be nought; by all which He indicates their plentifulness, and the infinity of His abundance.

But of what manner of light is He speaking, and what can this Light be? Not this that is sensible;

but another far better, which shews us heaven, the Angels, the Archangels, the Cherubim, the Seraphim, the Thrones, the Dominions, the Principalities, the Powers, the whole Host, the royal Palaces, the Tabernacles. For shouldest thou be counted worthy of this Light, thou shalt both see these, and be delivered from hell and from the venomous worm, and from the gnashing of teeth, and from the bonds that cannot be broken, and from the anguish and affliction, from the darkness that hath no light, and from being cut asunder, and from the river of fire, and from the curse, and from the abodes of sorrow; and thou shalt depart, "where sorrow and woe are fled away," where great is the joy and the peace, and the love, and the pleasure and the mirth; where is life eternal, and unspeakable glory, and inexpressible beauty; where are eternal tabernacles, and the untold glory of the King, and "those good things, which eye hath not seen, nor ear heard, neither have entered into the heart of man;" where is the spiritual bride-chamber, and the apartments of the heavens, and the virgins that bear the bright lamps, and they who have the marriage garment; where many are the possessions of our Lord, and the store-houses of the King.

Seest thou how great the rewards, and how many He hath set forth by one expression, and how He brought all together.

So also by unfolding each of the expressions that follow, we shall find our abundance great, and the ocean immense. Shall we then still delay, I beg you; and be backward to shew mercy on them that are in need? Nay I intreat, but though we must throw away all, be cast into the fire, venture against the sword, leap upon daggers, suffer what you will; let us bear all easily, that we may obtain the garment of the kingdom of heaven, and that untold glory; which may we all attain, by the grace and love towards man of our Lord Jesus Christ, to Whom be glory and might, world without end. Amen.

Homil. in S. Matt., liv.

Wednesday in Holy Week.

THE KING OF THE JEWS. S. AUGUSTINE.

"AND bearing His own Cross He went forth into a place called the place of Calvary, where they crucified Him."

He was going to the place where He was to be crucified, Jesus, bearing His own Cross! A great spectacle! but then to impiety a great disport to look upon; to piety a great mystery; impiety sees in it a great display of ignominy; piety a great strengthening of faith; impiety looks on, and laughs at a King bearing, instead of the rod of sovereignty, the wood of His punishment; piety looks on and sees the King bearing that Cross for Himself to be fixed thereon, which He would thereafter fix on the brows of kings; an object of contempt in the eyes of the impious, in that same thing in which thereafter the hearts of the saints should glory. Thus to Paul who should one day say, "But God forbid that I should glory, save in the Cross of our Lord Jesus Christ," the Lord commended that very Cross by bearing it on His Shoulders; and for that candle which was to be lighted, and not to be put under a bushel, the Lord bore the candlestick. Well then, "He bearing His own Cross went forth into a place called the place of Calvary, in the Hebrew Golgotha: where they crucified Him, and two other with Him, on either side one, and Jesus in the midst." These were the two thieves between whom He was fixed: He of Whom the prophecy which went before had said, "And He was numbered with the wicked."

"And Pilate wrote a title and put it on the Cross. And the writing was, Jesus of Nazareth, the King of the Jews. This title then read many of the Jews: for the place where Jesus was crucified was nigh to the city; and it was written in Hebrew, and Greek, and Latin." These three tongues, namely, were eminent before all others; the Hebrew because of the Jews who gloried in God's Law; the Greek because of the wise men of the Gentiles; the Latin, because of the Romans, at that time bearing rule over many, and indeed almost all nations.

"Then said the chief priests of the Jews to Pilate, Write not, The King of the Jews; but that He said, I am the King of the Jews. Pilate answered, What

I have written I have written." O ineffable power of the working of God even in the heart of the ignorant! Did not some hidden voice in the heart of Pilate inwardly, with (if one may so say) a sort of loud-voiced silence, make that to be heard, which so long time before was prophesied in the writing of the Psalms, "Destroy not the inscription of the title[1]." Behold, he does not destroy the inscription of the title, what he hath written, he hath written. But even the chief priests who wished this to be destroyed what said they? "Write not," say they, "the King of the Jews, but that He said, I am the King of the Jews." What speak ye, ye madmen? Why do ye gainsay the doing of that which ye can in no wise change? For shall it therefore be not true, because Jesus said, "I am the King of the Jews?" If that cannot be destroyed which Pilate hath written, can that be destroyed which the Truth hath spoken? But is Christ King of the Jews only, or also of the Gentiles? Yea, of the Gentiles also. For when He had said in the prophecy, "But I am set by Him as King upon Zion, His holy mountain, preaching the precepts of the Lord," (Ps. ii. 6,) lest on account of the Mount Zion, any should say that He was set as King only of the Jews, He hath straightway subjoined, "The Lord hath said unto Me, Thou art My Son, this day have I begotten Thee. Ask of Me, and I shall give Thee the heathen for Thine inheritance, and the uttermost parts of the earth for Thy possession." Whence also Himself by His own

[1] "Al-tas-chith." The title of Ps. lvii. lviii.

mouth, speaking among the Jews, saith, "And other sheep I have, which are not of this fold; them also I must bring, and they shall hear My Voice; and there shall be one fold, and One Shepherd." Why then would we have a great mystery to be understood in this title, in which it was written, "The King of the Jews," if Christ is King of the Gentiles also? Because truly the wild olive is made partaker of the fatness of the olive, not the olive made partaker of the bitterness of the wild olive. For in that the title was written according to truth concerning Christ, "The King of the Jews," what Jews are to be understood but the seed of Abraham, the sons of promise, who are also sons of God? Since, "Not they who are sons of the flesh," saith the Apostle, "these are the sons of God; but they who are sons of promise are counted for the seed." (Rom. ix. 1, 8.) And those were Gentiles to whom he said, "But if ye are Christ's, then are ye Abraham's seed, heirs according to the promise." (Gal. iii. 29.) King therefore of the Jews is Christ, but of the Jews who are such. "by circumcision of the heart, in the spirit, not in the letter; whose praise is not of men, but of God," (Rom. ii. 29;) of them who belong to the "Jerusalem which is free, our Mother eternal in the heavens," (Gal. iv. 22—31;) the spiritual Sarah, who casts from the house of liberty the bondwoman and her sons. For therefore, what Pilate hath written, he hath written; because what the Lord hath said He hath said.

Homil. in S. Joannis, cxvii.

Maundy Thursday.

CHRIST WASHING THE DISCIPLES' FEET. S. AUGUSTINE.

"HE riseth from supper, and layeth aside His garments, and took a towel, and girded Himself. After that He poureth water into a basin, and began to wash the disciples' feet, and to wipe them with the towel wherewith He was girded." What marvel that He rose from supper and laid aside His garments, "Who, being in the form of God, emptied Himself?" (Phil. ii. 6, 7.) And what marvel that He poured water into a basin wherewith to wash the disciples' feet, Who shed His Blood upon the earth wherewith to wash out the filthiness of sins? What marvel that with the towel wherewith He was girded He wiped the feet He had washed, Who by the flesh He had put on confirmed the footsteps of the Evangelists. And truly that He might gird Himself with the towel, He laid aside the garments He had on: but that He might take upon Him the form of a servant, when He emptied Himself, not what He had He laid aside, but what He had not, took. About to be crucified, He was stripped indeed of His garments, and being dead, was wrapped in linen cloths, and all that Passion of His is our cleansing. Being then to suffer the extreme of man's hatred,

He first performed the lowly services of love, not only to them for whom He was about to undergo death, but even to him who was about to deliver Him up unto death. So great truly is the benefit of man's lowliness, that even God's loftiness was pleased to enforce it by His own pattern: because proud man should be for ever lost, had not a lowly God found him. "For the Son of Man came to seek and to save that which was lost." Lost by following the pride of the deceiver, let him follow the lowliness of the Redeemer, being found.

When the Lord washed the feet of the disciples, "He cometh to Simon Peter: and Peter saith unto Him, Lord, dost Thou wash my feet?" For who would not shrink back in dismay from having his feet washed by the Son of God? Although therefore it was great audacity for a servant to gainsay his Lord, a man his God, yet Peter chose rather to do this than suffer his feet to be washed by his Lord and his God. "But Jesus answered and said unto him, What I do thou knowest not now, but thou shalt know hereafter." And still will not he, dismayed by the depth of the Lord's action, permit that to be done, which, why it was done, he knew not: but that Christ should be low even at his feet, as yet he will not see it done, he cannot bear it. "Thou shalt not wash my feet for ever," he saith.

Then the Saviour scaring the sick man out of his reluctance with the peril of his salvation, saith, "If I wash thee not, thou wilt have no part with Me." That it is said, "If I wash thee not," in a matter which concerned only the feet, is just as people use to say, "Thou treadest on *me*," when it is but the foot that is trodden upon. But he, in the perturbation of love and fear, and more dismayed by the thought of Christ denied him, than of Christ humbled even to his feet, saith, " Lord, not my feet only, but also my hands and my head!"

Since upon this threat Thou dost enforce it that my members must needs be washed by Thee, not only the lowest do I not draw from under Thy Hands, but the chiefest I lay down beneath Thy Feet. Lest Thou deny it me that I should have any part with Thee, I deny it not to Thee, that Thou shouldest wash any part of my body.

"Jesus saith unto Him, He that is washed, needeth not save to wash his feet, but is clean every whit." Here perchance some one may be staggered, and say, "Nay, if he is clean every whit, what need man to wash his feet?" But the Lord knew what He was saying, although our infirmity cannot penetrate His secrets.

But what is this? what does it mean? The Lord saith it, the Truth speaketh it, that one needeth to wash his feet, even he that is washed. What should it be, my brethren, but that the man in holy baptism indeed, is washed every whit, not "except the feet," but the whole man altogether: yet seeing thereafter one has to live in the midst of human affairs, of course one treads upon the earth. Therefore our human affections themselves, without which in this mortal state we cannot live, are as the feet wherein we are affected by human affairs, and so affected that "if we say we have no sin we deceive ourselves, and the truth is not in us." Every day therefore He washeth our feet Who intercedeth for us; and that we do every day need to wash our feet, that is, to direct the way of our spiritual steps, we confess also in the Lord's Prayer, when we say, "Forgive us our debts, as we forgive our debtors." For "If," as it is written, "we confess our sins," doubtless He Who washed the feet of His disciples "is faithful and just to forgive us our sins, and to cleanse us from all unrighteousness," that is, even to the feet, wherewith we move to and fro on earth.

Accordingly the Church which Christ cleanseth with the laver of water in the word, is not only in them without spot or wrinkle, who after the laver of regeneration are forthwith taken from the contagion of this life, and do not tread upon the earth that they should need to wash their feet; but also in them whom the Lord, affording them this mercy, hath made to depart from this world with feet also washen. But as for these who tarry here, albeit in them she be clean, because they live righteously, yet they have need to wash their feet, because without sin in any wise they are not.

We have learnt, my brethren, lowliness from the Most High, let us lowly do one to another, what was lowly done by the Most High. Great is this commendation of humility, and hereunto we are taught this lesson also, in the depth of meaning which is in this action of the Lord, that we should pray each for other, even as Christ maketh intercession for us. For if He Who neither hath, nor had, nor will have, any sin, prayeth for our sins, how much more ought we to pray for our sins, each for other? And if He forgiveth our sins, how much more ought we to forgive each other, who cannot live here without sin? For what doth the Lord seem to signify in this depth of inward and spiritual meaning, when He saith, "I have given you an example, that ye should do as I have done unto you," save what the Apostle saith most openly, "Forgiving one another, if any man have a quarrel against any; as the Lord hath forgiven you, so also do ye?" Let us then forgive one another his sins, and for our sins pray one for another, and so in some sort wash one another's feet.

On S. John. Hom. lv., lvi., and lviii.

Good Friday.

THE CRUCIFIXION. S. Cyril Jer.

"Who hath believed our report? and to whom is the arm of the Lord revealed? ... He is brought as a lamb to the slaughter, and as a sheep before her shearers is dumb, so He openeth not His mouth." Isa. liii. 1—7.

Every deed of Christ is a boast of the Catholic

Church, but her boast of boasts is the Cross, and knowing this, Paul says, "But God forbid that I should glory, save in the Cross of Christ." For wondrous indeed it was, that he who was blind from his birth should recover his sight in Siloam, but what is this compared with the blind of the whole world? It was a great thing and passing nature for Lazarus to rise again after four days, but this grace extended to him alone, and what was it compared with the dead in sin throughout the whole world? Marvellous was it that five loaves should issue forth into food for the five thousand; but what is that to those who are famishing in ignorance through all the world? It was marvellous that she should have been loosed who had been bound by Satan eighteen years; yet what is this to all of us, who are fast bound in the chains of our sins? Now the glory of the Cross has led into light those who were blind through ignorance, has loosed all who were held fast by sin, and has ransomed the whole world of men.

And wonder not that the whole world was ransomed; for it was no mere man, but the Only-Begotten Son of God Who died on its behalf. And yet one man's sin, even Adam's, had power to bring death to the world: but "if by one man's offence death reigned" over the world, how shall not life much rather reign "by the Righteousness of One?" And if because of the tree of food they were then cast out of Paradise, shall not believers now because of the Tree of Jesus, much more easily enter into Paradise? If the first man formed out of the earth brought in universal death, shall not He Who formed him out of the earth bring in everlasting life, being Himself Life? If Phinees when he waxed zealous, and slew the evil-doer, stopped the wrath of God, shall not Jesus, Who slew not another, but gave up Himself for a ransom, put away the wrath which is against men?

Let us then not be ashamed of the Cross of our Saviour, but rather glory in it. "For the preaching of the Cross is unto the Jews a stumbling-block, and unto the Greeks foolishness," but to us salvation; and "to them that perish it is foolishness, but unto us which are saved it is the power of God." For it was not a mere man Who died for us, as I said before, but the Son of God, God made Man. Further, if under Moses a lamb kept the destroyer at a distance, did not much rather the "Lamb of God, which taketh away the sins of the world," deliver us from our sins? The blood of a brute animal gave salvation and shall not the Blood of the Only-Begotten much rather save? If any disbelieve the power of the Crucified, let him enquire of the devils; if any believe not words, let him believe what he sees. Many have been crucified throughout the world, but by none of these are the devils scared; but Christ having been crucified for us, when they see but the sign of the Cross, they shudder. For those died for their own sins, but Christ for the sins of others; for He "did no sin, neither was guile found in His mouth." It is not Peter who says this, for then we might suspect that He was partial to his Teacher, but it is Esaias who says it, not indeed present with Him in the flesh, but in the Spirit contemplating aforetime His coming in the flesh. Yet why now bring the Prophet only as a witness? receive the witness of Pilate himself who gave sentence upon Him saying, "I find no fault in this Man:" and who, when He gave Him up, washed his hands and said, "I am innocent of the blood of this Just Person." There is yet another witness of the sinlessness of Jesus, the robber, the first man admitted into Paradise; who rebuked his fellow, and said, "We receive the due reward of our deeds; but this Man hath done nothing amiss; for we were present, both thou and I, at His judgment."

Jesus then really suffered for all men: for the Cross was no illusion, otherwise our Redemption is an illusion also. His Death was not in appearance, for then is our salvation also a tale. Being then in the flesh like others, He was crucified, but not for like sins. For He was not led to death for covetousness, in that He was the Teacher of poverty; not for smiting or striking hastily, for He turned the other cheek also to the smiter; not for despising the Law, for He was the Fulfiller of the Law; not for reviling a prophet, for it was Himself Who was proclaimed by the prophets; not for defrauding any of their line, for He ministered without reward and freely. He sinned not in words, or deeds, or thoughts, "Who did no sin, neither was guile found in His mouth; Who when He was reviled, reviled not again; when He suffered, He threatened not;" Who came to His Passion, not unwillingly, but willingly, yea, should any dissuading Him say even now, "Be it far from Thee, Lord," He will say again, "Get thee behind Me, Satan."

And wouldest thou be persuaded that He came to His Passion willingly? others die without their own will, in that they know not of their death; but He spoke before of His Passion. "Behold, the Son of man is betrayed to be crucified." But knowest thou wherefore this Friend of man shunned not death? It was lest the whole world should perish in its sins. "Behold, we go up to Jerusalem, and the Son of man shall be betrayed, and shall be crucified;" and again, "He stedfastly set His face to go to Jerusalem." And wouldest thou know certainly, that the Cross is a glory to Jesus? Hear His own words, not mine. Judas set about betraying Him, being ungrateful to the Master of the house. Having but just now gone forth from His Table, and drunk His Cup of blessing, yet in return for that draught of salvation he sought to shed righteous blood. "He who did eat of His Bread lifted up his heel against Him;" his hands were but lately receiving the blessed gifts, and within a little while for the wages of treason he was plotting His death. And being reproved, and having heard that word, "Thou hast said," he again went out. Then said Jesus, "The hour is come, that the Son of Man should be glorified." Thou seest how He knew the Cross to be His proper glory. Further, was Esaias when he was sawn asunder not ashamed, and shall Christ be ashamed when dying for the world? "Now is the Son of Man glorified:" not but that He had glory before; for He was "glorified with the glory" which was before the foundation of the world. He was glorified as God ever, but now He was glorified in bearing the Crown of His patience. He gave not up His Life by force, nor was He put to death violently, but of His own accord. Hear what He says: "I have power to lay down My Life, and I have power to take it again:" I yield it of My own choice to My enemies, for unless I chose, this could not be. He came therefore of His own set purpose to His Passion, rejoicing in His noble deed, smiling at the crown, cheered by the salvation of men: not ashamed of the Cross, for it saved the world. For it was no common man who suffered, but God in man's nature, striving for the prize of His patience.

Let us seek the texts in proof of the Passion of Christ: for we are met together, not now to make an abstract exposition of the Scripture, but rather to be made assured of the things which we already believe. Now therefore I begin from whence the Passion began. Judas was the traitor who came against Him, and stood, and speaking words of peace, and plotting war. The Psalmist then says concerning Him, "My friends and My neighbours drew near against Me, and stood." And again, "His words were softer than oil, yet were they drawn swords." "Hail, Master," and he betrayed his Master to death; he was not moved with His warning when He said, "Judas, betrayest thou the Son of man with a kiss?" saying as it were this to him; Recollect thine own name; Judas means confession; thou hast come to terms, thou hast received the money, make confession quickly. "Hold not Thy peace, O God of My praise; for the wicked and the mouth of the deceitful are opened against Me; they have spoken against Me with a lying tongue, they have compassed Me about also with words of hatred." But that some of the chief priests also were present, and that the bonds were before the gate of the city, thou hast heard before, if thou rememberest the exposition of the Psalmist, who has told the time and place, how "they returned at evening, and hungered like dogs, and encompassed the city." (Ps. lix. 6. Sept.)

Attend also in respect to the thirty pieces of silver. "And I will say to them, If it be good in your sight, give me my price, or refuse," &c. (Zech. xi. 12. Sept.) One price is owing to Me from you for My healing the blind and lame, and I receive another; for thanksgiving, dishonour; for worship, insult. Beholdest thou how the Scripture foresaw these things? "And they appointed My price at thirty pieces of silver." (Ibid.) How exact the prophecy! how great and unerring is the wisdom of the Holy Ghost! For he said, not ten, nor twenty, but thirty; exactly as many as there were. Tell also what became of this value, O Prophet! Does he who received it keep it, or does he restore it? and after it was restored, what becomes of it? The Prophet then says, "And I took the thirty pieces of silver, and cast them into the House of the Lord, into the refining house." Zech. xi. 13. Sept.) Compare the Gospel with the prophecy, " Judas," it says, "repented himself and cast down the pieces of silver in the temple and departed."

Those conscientious Jews forsooth, the high-priests of that time, seeing Judas repenting and saying, " I have sinned in that I have betrayed the innocent blood," reply, " What is that to us? see thou to that." Is it then nothing to you, the crucifiers? but shall he who received and restored the price of murder, see to it, and shall the murderers not see to it? Then they say among themselves, "It is not lawful to cast them into the treasury, because it is the price of blood." Out of your own mouths is your condemnation; if the price is polluted, so is the deed polluted, but if thou art fulfilling righteousness in crucifying Christ, why receivest thou not the price of it?

They bound Jesus, and led Him to the hall of the high-priest. And wouldest thou know and be sure that this also is written? Esaias says, " Woe unto their soul, for they have taken evil counsel against themselves, saying, Let us bind the Just, for He is troublesome to us." (Isa. iii. 9, 10. Sept.) And truly, " Woe unto their soul!" Let us see how. Esaias was sawn asunder, yet after this the people was restored. Jeremias was cast into the mire of the dungeon, yet was the wound of the Jews healed; for it was the less, in that it was a sin against man. But when the Jews sinned, not against man, but against God in man's nature, "Woe unto their soul!" He says, " Let us bind the Just;" could He not then set Himself free? some one will say; He Who freed Lazarus from the bonds of death after four days, and loosed Peter from the iron bands of his prison. Angels stood around ready, saying, "Let us burst their bonds in sunder," but they held back, because their Lord was pleased to undergo it. Again, He was led to the judgment-seat before the elders; thou hast already the testimony to this, "The Lord will come into judgment with the ancients of His people, and the princes thereof." (Isa. iii. 14.)

And the high-priest having questioned Him, and heard the truth, is wroth: and the wicked minister of wicked men smites Him; and the Countenance, which had shone as the sun, endured to be smitten with lawless hands. Others coming spat on the Face of Him Who by His spittle had healed one who was blind from his birth. "Do ye thus requite the Lord, O foolish people and unwise?" (Deut. xxxii. 6.) And the Prophet wondering says, "Lord, who hath believed our report?" for the thing is incredible that God, the Son of God, and the Arm of the Lord, should suffer such things. But that they who are saved may not disbelieve, the Holy Ghost writes before, in the Person of Christ, Who says, (for He Who then spake these things, was afterwards an actor in them,) "I gave My back to the scourges;" for Pilate having scourged Him, delivered Him to be crucified; "and My cheeks to smitings, and My Face I turned not away from the shame of spittings," saying as it were, "Though knowing before that they would smite Me, I did not even turn My cheek aside: for how should I have warned My disciples against death for truth's sake, had I Myself sunk under this? I said, He who loveth his life shall lose it; if I had loved My life, how could I have taught, not doing what I taught?" First then, being Himself God, He endured to suffer these things at the hands of men; that after this we men, when we suffer such things at the hands of men for His sake, might not be ashamed.

Look with awe at the Lord while He was judged. He endured to be led and carried by the soldiers. Pilate sat in judgment, and He Who sitteth on the Right Hand of the Father, stood and was judged. The people whom He had redeemed from the land of Egypt, and oft-times from other places, shouted against Him, "Away with Him! away with Him! crucify Him!" Wherefore, O ye Jews? because He has healed the blind? or because He has made the lame to walk, and bestowed His other benefits? So that the Prophet in amazement speaks of this too. "Against whom have ye opened your mouth, and against whom have ye let loose your tongue?" And the Lord Himself says in the Prophets, "Mine heritage is unto Me as a lion in the forest; it crieth out against Me, therefore have I hated it." I have not refused them, but they have refused Me; wherefore it follows that I say, "I have forsaken My house."

When He was judged, He held His peace; so that Pilate was moved for Him, and said, "Hearest Thou not what these witness against Thee?" Not that he knew Him Who was judged, but he feared his own wife's dream. And Jesus held His peace. The Psalmist says, "I was as a man that heareth not; and in whose mouth are no reproofs;" and again, "But I as a deaf man heard not; and I was as a dumb man that openeth not his mouth."

But the soldiers who surrounded Him, mock Him, and their Lord becomes a sport to them, and their Master is turned into jest by them. "When they looked on Me, they shaked their heads." (Ps. cix. 25.) Yet there is the figure of kingly state, for though they mock, yet do they bend the knee. And the soldiers crucify Him, having first put on Him a purple robe, and they set a crown on His Head; for what though it be of thorns? Every king is proclaimed by soldiers; it became Jesus too in a figure to have been crowned by soldiers; so that for this cause the Scripture says in the Canticles, "Go forth, O ye daughter of Zion, and behold King Solomon in the crown wherewith his mother crowned Him." (Cant. iii. 11.) And the crown itself was a mystery; for it was a remissal of sins, and dismissal of the curse.

The Lord was crucified, thou hast received the testimonies. Thou seest this spot of Golgotha[1]! Rejoice not in the Cross in time of peace only, but hold fast the same faith in time of persecution also; not being a friend of Jesus in time of peace, and His

---

[1] These lectures were preached at Jerusalem in the Basilica of Constantine called of the Holy Cross, and erected close to the Holy Sepulchre, within sight of the summit of Golgotha.

foe in time of wars. Thou receivest now the forgiveness of thy sins, and the gifts of the King's spiritual bounty; when war shall come, strive thou with high heart for thy King. Jesus, the Sinless, for thee was crucified; and wilt not thou be crucified for Him Who was crucified for thee? Thou art not bestowing a favour, repaying thy debt to Him Who in Golgotha was crucified for thee. Now Golgotha is interpreted, "the place of a skull." Who were they then, who prophetically named this Golgotha, in which Christ the true Head endured the Cross? As the Apostle says, "Who is the Image of the Invisible God;" and after a little, "And He is the Head of the body, the Church." And again, "The Head of every man is Christ." And again, "Who is the Head of all principality and power." The Head suffered, "in the place of the skull." O wondrous prophetic adaptation! The very name almost reminds thee, saying, "Think not of the Crucified as of a mere man; He is the Head of all principality and power. That Head which was crucified is the Head of all power, and has for His Head the Father; for the Head of the man is Christ, and the Head of Christ is God." (1 Cor. xi. 3.)

Christ then was crucified for us, having been judged in the night, when it was cold, and a fire of coals was laid. He was crucified at the third hour; and from the sixth hour there was darkness until the ninth hour; but from the ninth hour there was light again. He stretched out His Hands on the Cross that He might encompass the ends of the

world; He stretched forth human hands, Who by
His spiritual Hands had established the heaven;
and they were fastened with nails, that His Manhood
Which bore the sins of men, having been nailed to
the tree, and having died, sin might die with it and
we rise again in righteousness. "For since by one
man came death," by One Man also came life; by
One Man, the Saviour, dying of His own accord; for
remember what He said, "I have power to lay down
My life, and I have power to take it again."

So He endured all these things, having come for
the salvation of all; but the people returned Him
an evil recompence. Jesus says, "I thirst," He
Who had brought forth the waters for them out
of the flinty rock; and He asks fruit of the vine
which He had planted. But what does the vine?
This vine, by nature indeed of the holy fathers, but
of Sodom by purpose of heart; for "their vine is of
the vine of Sodom, and of the fields of Gomorrah,"
(Deut. xxxii. 32;) this vine, when the Lord was
athirst, having filled a sponge and put it on a reed,
offers Him vinegar. "They gave Me also gall for
My meat, and in My thirst they gave Me vinegar to
drink." (Ps. lxix. 21.) Thou seest the plainness of
the Prophet's description. Are these things what
ye recompense unto the Lord? offerest thou these
things, O vine, unto thy Master? Rightly did the
Prophet Esaias aforetime bewail you, saying, "My
well-beloved hath a vineyard in a very fruitful hill,"
and (not to recite the whole) he goes on, "I waited
that it should bring forth grapes;" I thirsted that it

should give wine; "but it brought forth thorns;" for thou seest the crown, wherewith I am adorned. What then shall I now decree? "I will command the clouds that they rain no rain upon it."

And concerning the robbers who were crucified with Him, it was written, "And He was numbered with the transgressors." Both of them had been transgressors, but one was so no longer; for the one was a transgressor to the end, stubborn against salvation, whose hands indeed were fastened, but who through his blasphemies smote with his tongue. When the Jews passing by wagged their heads, mocking the crucified, and fulfilling what was written, "When they looked on Me they shaked their heads," (Ps. cxx. 25) he also reviled with them. But the other rebuked the reviler; and to him the end of life was the beginning of restoration; the surrender of his soul was a preventing others in salvation. And after rebuking him, he says, "Lord, remember me;" for to Thee is my speech. Leave this man, for the eyes of his understanding are blinded; but remember me. I say not Remember my works, for of these I am afraid. Every man has a feeling for his fellow traveller; I am travelling with Thee deathwards; remember me, Thy fellow wayfarer. I say not Remember me now, but, "when Thou comest into Thy kingdom."

What power, O robber, enlightened thee? Who taught thee to worship that despised Man, thy companion on the Cross? O eternal light, which givest light to them that are in darkness! Therefore also he rightly heard the words, "Be of good cheer;" not that thy deeds are such as should make thee be of good cheer; but that the King is here, dispensing favours. The request reached unto a distant time, but the grace is very speedy. "Verily I say unto thee, This day shalt thou be with Me in Paradise;" because "to-day" thou hast "heard My voice" and hast not "hardened thine heart." Very speedily I passed sentence upon Adam, very speedily I pardon thee. To him it was said, "In the day wherein thou eatest, thou shalt surely die;" but thou to-day hast obeyed the faith, to-day is thy salvation. Adam by the Tree fell; thou by the Tree art brought to Paradise. Fear not the serpent; he shall not cast thee out; for he is fallen from heaven. And I say not unto thee, This day shalt thou depart; but, This day shalt thou be with Me. Be of good courage, thou shalt not be cast out. Fear not the fiery sword, it shrinks from its Lord. O mighty and ineffable grace! The faithful Abraham had not yet entered, and the lawless robber enters! Moses and the prophets had not yet entered, and the lawless robber enters. Paul also wondered at this before thee, saying, "where sin abounded, there grace did much more abound." They who had borne the burden and heat of the day had not yet entered; and he of the eleventh hour entered. Let none murmur against the good man of the house, for he says, "Friend, I do thee no wrong; is it not lawful for Me to do what I will with Mine Own?" The robber has a wish to work righteousness, but death prevents him;

I wait not exclusively for work, I have accepted faith. "I am come to feed My sheep among the lilies, I am come to feed My sheep in the gardens." (Cant. vi. 3.) I have found a sheep, a lost one, but I lay it on My shoulders, for he believes, since he himself has said, "I have gone astray like a lost sheep: Lord remember me when Thou comest in Thy kingdom."

Of this garden I sang of old to My spouse in the Canticles, and spoke thus to her. "I am come into My garden, My sister, My spouse;" (now the place where He was crucified was a garden;) and what takest Thou thence? "I have gathered My myrrh," having drunk wine mingled with myrrh, and vinegar. And having received these, He said, "It is finished." For the mystery has been fulfilled; the things that are written have been fulfilled; sins are forgiven. For "Christ being come an High-Priest of good things to come, by a greater and more perfect tabernacle, not made with hands, that is to say not of this building, neither by the blood of goats and calves, but by His own Blood, He entered in once into the holy Place, having obtained eternal redemption for us; for if the blood of bulls and of goats and the ashes of an heifer, sprinkling the unclean, sanctifieth to the purifying of the flesh, how much more the Blood of Christ?" And again, "Having therefore, brethren, boldness to enter into the holiest by the Blood of Jesus, by a new and living way, which He hath consecrated for us, through the veil, that is to say, His flesh." And because

His flesh, this veil, was dishonoured, the emblematical veil of the temple was rent through, as it is written, "And, behold, the veil of the temple was rent in twain from the top to the bottom;" for not a morsel of it was left; for since the Master said, "Behold your house is left unto you desolate," the house has been rent into pieces.

These things the Saviour endured, "making peace through the Blood of His Cross, for things in heaven, and things in earth." For we were enemies of God through sin, and God had appointed the sinner to die. There must needs therefore have happened one of two things; either that God, keeping His words, should destroy all men, or that in His loving-kindness, He should cancel the sentence. But behold the Wisdom of God; He preserved both to His sentence its truth, and to His loving-kindness its exercise. Christ took our sins "in His Body on the tree, that we being dead to sin, should live to righteousness." Of no small account was He Who died for us; He was not a literal sheep; He was not a mere man; He was more than an Angel; He was God made man. The transgression of sinners was not so great as the righteousness of Him Who died for them; we have not committed as much sin as He wrought righteousness, Who laid down His life for us, Who laid it down when He pleased, and took it again when He pleased. And wouldest thou have proof that He laid down His life not by violence, nor against His Will yielded up the Ghost? He cried to His Father, saying, "Father, into Thy hands, I commend My Spirit;" I commend it, that I may take it again. And having said these things, He gave up the Ghost; but not for any long time, for He rose again from the dead speedily.

The sun was darkened, because of the Sun of Righteousness. The rocks were rent, because of the Spiritual Rock. The tombs were opened, and the dead arose, because of Him Who was "free among the dead; He sent forth His prisoners out of the pit wherein is no water." (Ps. lxxx. 5; Zech. ix. 4.) Be not then ashamed of the Crucified, but be thyself bold to say, "He beareth our sins, and carrieth our sorrows, and with His stripes we are healed." Let us not be unthankful to our Benefactor. And again, "for the transgression of my people was He stricken, and He made His grave with the wicked, and with the rich in His Death." Therefore Paul says plainly, "that Christ died for our sins according to the Scriptures, and that He rose again the third day according to the Scriptures."

But we seek to be told plainly where He has been buried. Is His tomb then made with hands? The Prophets say, "Look unto the solid rock which ye have hewn. Look and behold." (Isa. li. 1. Sept.) Thou hast in the Gospel, "In a sepulchre hewn in stone, which was hewn out of a rock." What kind of door has the sepulchre? Again another Prophet says, "They cut off My life in the dungeon, and cast a stone upon Me." (Lam. iii. 53.) I Who am "the chief Corner-stone, elect, precious," lie for a little time within a stone. I Who am a stone of stumbling to the Jews, but of salvation to them who believe. The Tree of Life, therefore, was planted in the earth, that the earth which had been cursed might enjoy the blessing, and that the dead might be released.

Let us not then be ashamed to confess the Crucified. Be the Cross our seal made with boldness by our fingers on our brow, and in every thing: even the bread we eat, and the cups we drink; in our comings in, and goings out; before our sleep, when we lie down and when we awake; when we are in the way, and when we are still. Great is that preservative: it is without price for the poor's sake, without toil for the sick; since also its grace is from God. It is the sign of the faithful, and the dread of devils; for he has "triumphed over them in it, having made a show of them openly;" for when they see the Cross, they are reminded of the Crucified; they are afraid of Him; they are afraid of Him, Who hath "bruised the heads of the dragon." Despise not the Seal because of the freeness of the gift; but for this the rather honour thy Benefactor. Take therefore first as an unassailable foundation, the Cross, and build upon it the rest of thy faith. This shall appear again with Jesus from heaven; for the trophy shall precede the King: that seeing "Him Whom they pierced," and by the Cross knowing Him Who was dishonoured, the Jews may repent and mourn, and that we may glory, boasting of the Cross, worshipping the Lord Who was sent, and Crucified for us, and worshipping also God His

Father Who sent Him, with the Holy Ghost; to Whom be glory for ever and ever. Amen.

Catechet. Lect., xiii.

Easter Eve.

WATCHING. S. EPHREM.

WHO would pass this night in slumber? . . . . . Watch not we as usurers, who, on money put to interest thinking, watch at night so oft, to reckon up their capital and interest. Waking, full of cool devices, is t e thief, who in the earth hath buried and concealed his sleep. His wakefulness all ends in this, that he may cause much wakefulness to them that be asleep. Wakeful likewise is the glutton, who hath eaten much and is restless; his watching is to him torment, because of stint he was impatient. Wakeful likewise is the merchant; of a night he works his fingers telling o'er what pounds are coming, and if his wealth doubles or trebles. Wakeful likewise is the rich man, whose sleep his riches chase away: his dogs are sleeping, he doth guard his treasures from the thieves. Wakeful also is the careful, by his care his sleep is swallowed: though his end standeth by his pillow, yet he wakes with cares for years to come. Satan teacheth, O my brethren, in one watching's stead another, that to good deeds we be sleepy, and to ill awake and watchful. Even Judas Iscariot for the whole night through was wakeful, and he sold the Righteous Blood, that did purchase the whole world. The son of the dark one put on darkness, having stripped the light from off him; and the Creator of silver, for silver the thief did sell. Yea Pharisees, the dark one's sons, all the night through kept awake; the dark ones watched that they might veil the light which is unlimited. Ye then watch as heaven's lights in this night of starry light. For though so dark its colour is, yet in virture it is clear.

For whoever is like this clear One, wakeful and at prayer in darkness, in this darkness visible him a light unseen envelopes! The bad man that in daylight standeth, yet as a son of darkness dealeth, though with light clad outwardly, inly is with darkness girt. Be we not deceived, beloved, by the fact that we are watching! For whoso doth not rightly watch, his watch is an unrighteous watch. Whoso watcheth not cheerfully, his watching but a sleeping is: whoso also watcheth not innocently, even his waking is his foe. This is the waking of the envious one! a solid mass, compact with harm. That watch is but a trafficking with scorn and mockery compact. The wrathful man if he doth wake, fretful with wrath his wake will be, and his watching proves to him full of rage and of cursings. If the babbler be watching, then his mouth becomes a passage which for sins is expeditious, but for prayers disrelish shews.

The wise man if so be that he watches, one of two things chooseth him, either he takes sweet, moderate sleep, or a holy vigil keeps. That night is fair, wherein the Fair One rose to come and make us fair. Let not aught that may disturb it enter into our watch. Fair be kept the ear's approach, chaste the seeing of the eye! hallowed the musing of the heart! speaking of the mouth be cleared. . . . .

In this night of reconcilement, let no man be wroth or gloomy! In this night that stilleth all, none that threateneth or disturbs! This night belongeth to the Sweet One; bitter none, nor harsh be in it! In this night that is the Meek One's, high or haughty none be in it! In this day of pardoning, let us not be unforgiving! (In this day of gladnesses, let us not spread sadnesses! In this day so sweet, let not us be harsh!) In this day of peaceful rest, let us not be wrathful! 'Tis to-day that opened for us a gate on high to our prayers.

The Rhythms of S. Ephrem on the Nativity, i.

www.ingramcontent.com/pod-product-compliance
Lightning Source LLC
Chambersburg PA
CBHW031938230426
43672CB00010B/1966